A Garland Series

The English Stage
Attack and Defense 1577 - 1730

A collection of 90 important works
reprinted in photo-facsimile in 50 volumes

edited by
Arthur Freeman
Boston University

Historia Histrionica

An Historical Account of the English-Stage

by

James Wright

Roscius Anglicanus

Or an Historical Review of the Stage

by

John Downes

with a preface
for the Garland Edition by

Arthur Freeman

Garland Publishing, Inc., New York & London

1974

Library of Congress Cataloging in Publication Data

Wright, James, 1643-1713.
    Historia histrionica.

    (The English stage: attack and defense, 1577-1730,
v. 38)
    Reprint of the 1699 ed. of Historia histrionica
printed by G. Groom for W. Haws, London (Wing W3695),
and of the 1708 ed. of Roscius Anglicanus, printed by
H. Playford, London.
    1. Theater--England--History. I. Downes, John,
fl. 1662-1710. Roscius Anglicanus. 1974. II. Title.
III. Title: Roscius Anglicanus. IV. Series.
PN2585.W68   1974b   792'.0942   70-170465
ISBN 0-8240-0621-6

Printed in the United States of America

Preface

These two anonymous theatrical histories are among the most important accounts of the English stage, ranking between them perhaps second only to Langbaine, and of course far superseding Langbaine in their disclosures of actors and theatres, companies and repertory performance.

James Wright's shorter tract, set as an entertaining dialogue between a "modern" playgoer and an old cavalier — a kind of 1699 equivalent of Ben Jonson's reactionary spectator of Bartholomew Fair *(1614) — contains a startling amount of oral history, preserved no doubt as gossip, but also probably deriving from Wright's personal acquaintance with such actors as the "superannuated" John Lowin, whose career began about 1602, but who was running a London tavern as late as 1669. Wright himself was born in 1643, and his career as an antiquary is certainly bound up with his collecting of early dramatic quartos and manuscripts, signaled by Thomas Hearne (1713) as "one*

5

of the finest collections of old plays since Cart-wright" (cf. W.W. Greg, Bibliography of the English Printed Drama, *III, 1306 ff.). Wright's old playgoer, Truman, claims familiarity with the stage of the 1630s, and, by report, of even earlier decades. John Heming "and others of the Older sort, were Dead before I knew the Town," he explains, and Heming died in 1630. He describes Alleyn's activities from hearsay, and from apparent knowledge five playhouses, many actors, and many performances, with parts and players identified. On the whole Wright's remarkable reconstruction has proved reliable, and is generally cited with minimal caution as one of the very few pieces of printed evidence we possess relative to the actual style of performance and popularity of the pre-restoration actors and houses.*

Historia Histrionica *appears in the Term Catalogues for June, 1699 (III, 143), and was advertised in* The Post Boy *for 4-6 July (Hooker). Wing incomprehensibly lists an edition of 1656 (W 3694, no imprint, Oxford only), when Wright would have been thirteen years old; I have not pursued this. At the suggestion of Thomas Wharton, Robert Dodsley included the piece in the penultimate volume of his* Old Plays *(1744 and all further editions;*

6

PREFACE

not 1774, and volume XI, not II, as in Lowe-Arnott-Robinson); there were other edited reprints in 1750 (Dodsley's edition of Cibber's Apology; *also in later editions), 1830, and 1872; extracts appear in* Social England Illustrated *(1903) and in Bentley's* Jacobean and Caroline Stage, *II, 691-6.*

John Downes was prompter to the Duke's Servants, the Restoration company with which Sir William D'Avenant opened the Lincoln's Inn Fields theatre in 1662, and to his Roscius Anglicanus *we owe most of our imperfect knowledge of the operation of the Restoration stage. As a text it has long been esteemed and frequently reprinted, but rarely from the 1708 original. An edition "with additions, by the late Thomas Davies," prepared by F.G. Waldron, appeared in the latter's curious* Literary Museum *(1789; collected with other pieces 1792); a "reprint" in 125 copies was issued by Joseph Knight, the author of the* DNB *account of Downes, in 1886; and an edition with notes by Montague Summers was published by the Fortune Press in 1928; this latter version is the basis of Benjamin Blom's recent reprint (New York, 1968).*

Our reprint of Wright's Historia Histrionica *is made from the 1699 original, The Harvard University copy (Thr 408.8*), collating A^4 (A1*

7

PREFACE

blank)B-E[4]. *The copy for* Roscius Anglicanus *is the 1708 first edition, the Folger copy (PN2592 D6), collating* $A^2 B-D^8 E^2$. *Lowe-Arnott-Robinson 822 and 824.*

February, 1973   A. F.

HISTORIA HISTRIONICA:

A N

Hiſtorical Account

OF THE

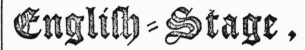

SHEWING

The ancient Uſe, Improvement, and Perfection, of Dramatick Repreſentations, in this Nation.

IN A

Dialogue, of *PLAYS* and *PLAYERS*.

―― *Olim meminiſſe juvabit.*

LONDON.

Printed by *G. Croom*, for *William Haws* at the Roſe in *Ludgate-ſtreet.* 1699.

THE
PREFACE.

Much has been Writ of late pro *and* con, *about the Stage, yet the Subject admits of more, and that which has not been hetherto toucht upon; not only what that is, but what it was, about which some People have made such a Busle. What it is we see, and I think it has been sufficiently display'd in Mr.* Collier's *Book; What it was in former Ages, and how used in this Kingdom, so far back as one may collect any Memorialls, is the Subject of the following*

The PREFACE.

ing *Dialogue.* Old *Plays* will be always *Read by the* Curious, *if it were only to discover the Manners and Behaviour of several Ages; and how they alter'd.* For *Plays are exactly like* Portraits *Drawn in the Garb and Fashion of the time when* Painted. *You see one Habit in the time of King* Charles I. *another quite different from that, both for Men and Women, in* Queen Eli-zabeths *time another; under* Henry *the Eighth different from both; and so backward all various. And in the several Fashions of Behaviour and Conversation, there is as much Mutability as in that of Cloaths.* Reli-gion *and Religious matters was once as much the Mode in publick Enter-tainments, as the Contrary has been*

in

The PREFACE.

*in some times since. This appears
in the different Plays of several Ages:
And to evince this, the following
Sheets are an Essay or Specimen.*

*Some may think the Subject of this
Discourse trivial, and the persons
herein mention'd not worth remember-
ing. But besides that I could name
some things contested of late with
great heat, of as little, or less Conse-
quence, the Reader may know that
the Profession of Players is not so
totally scandalous, nor all of them so
reprobate, but that there has been
found under that Name, a Canonized
Saint in the primitive Church; as
may be seen in the* Roman Martyrology *on the* 29th *of* March; *his
name* Masculas *a Master of Interludes,* (*the Latin is* Archimimus,
and*

and the French Translation **un Maitre Comedien**) *who under the Persecution of the* **Vandals** *in* **Africa**, *by* Geifericus *the* **Arian King**, *having endured many and greivious Torments and Reproaches for the Confeffion of the* **Truth**, *finifht the Courfe of this glorious Combat. Saith the faid* **Martyrology**.

It appears from this, and fome further Inftances in the following Difcourfe, That there have been **Players** *of worthy* **Principles** *as to* **Religion**, **Loyalty**, *and other* **Virtues**; *and if the major part of them fall under a different* **Character**, *it is the general unhappinefs of* **Mankind**, *that the* **Moft** *are the* **Worft**.

A

A
DIALOGUE
OF
PLAYS and *PLAYERS.*

Lovewit, Truman.

Lovew. Honeſt Old Cavalier! well met, 'faith I'm glad to ſee thee.

Trum Have a care what you call me. Old, is a Word of Diſgrace among the Ladies ; to be Honeſt is to be Poor and Fooliſh, (as ſome think) and Cavalier is a Word as much out of Faſhion as any of 'em.

Lovew. The more's the pity : But what ſaid the Fortune-Teller in *Ben. Johnſon*'s Mask of *Gypſies,* to the then *Lord Privy Seal,*

Honeſt and Old !
In thoſe the Good Part of a Fortune is told.

B *Trum.*

Trum. *Ben. Johnson?* How dare you name *Ben. Johnson* in thefe times? When we have fuch a crowd of Poets of a quite different Genius; the leaft of which thinks himfelf as well able to correct *Ben. Johnson*, as he could a Country School Miftrefs that taught to Spell.

Lovew. We have indeed, Poets of a different Genius; fo are the Plays: But in my Opinion, they are all of 'em (fome few excepted) as much inferior to thofe of former Times, as the Actors now in being (generally fpeaking) are, compared to *Hart*, *Mohun*, *Burt*, *Lacy*, *Clun*, and *Shatterel*; for I can reach no farther backward.

Trum. I can; and dare affure you, if my Fancy and Memory are not partial (for Men of my Age are apt to be over indulgent to the thoughts of their youthful Days) I fay the Actors that I have feen before the Wars, *Lowin*, *Tayler*, *Pollard*, and fome others, were almoft as far beyond *Hart* and his Company, as thofe were beyond thefe now in being.

Lovew. I am willing to believe it, but cannot readily; becaufe I have been told, That thofe whom I mention'd, were Bred up under the others of your Acquaintance, and follow'd their manner of Action, which is now loft. So far, that when the Queftion has been askt, Why thefe Players do not receive the *Silent Woman*, and fome other of *Johnson*'s Plays, (once of higheft efteem) they have anfwer'd, truly, Becaufe there are none now Living who can

rightly

rightly Humour thofe Parts, for all who re-
lated to the *Black-friers* (where they were
Acted in perfection) are now Dead, and almoft forgotten.

Trum. 'Tis very true, *Hart* and *Clun*, were
bred up Boys at the *Blackfriers*; and Acted
Womens Parts, *Hart* was *Robinfon*'s Boy or
Apprentice : He Acted the Dutchefs in the
Tragedy of *the Cardinal,* which was the fiſt
Part that gave him Reputation. *Cartwright,*
and *Winterſhal* belong'd to the private Houſe
in *Salisbury-Court, Bart* was a Boy firſt under
Shank at the *Black-friers,* then under *Beeſton* at
the *Cockpit*; and *Mohun*, and *Shatterel* were
in the fame Condition with him, at the laſt
Place. There *Burt* uſed to Play the principal
Women's Parts, in particular *Clariana* in *Love's
Cruelty*; and at the fame time *Mohun* Acted *Bella-
mente,* which Part he retain'd after the Reſtau-
ration.

Lovew. That I have feen, and can well remember. I wiſh they had Printed in the laſt
Age (fo I call the times before the Rebellion)
the Actors Names over againſt the Parts they
Acted, as they have done fince the Reſtaurati-
on. And thus one might have gueſt at the
Action of the Men, by the Parts which we
now Read in the Old Plays.

Trum. It was not the Cuſtome and Uſage
of thofe Days, as it hath been fince. Yet
fome few Old Plays there are that have the
Names fet againſt the Parts, as, *The Dutchefs*

of

of *Malfy*; the *Picture*; the *Roman Actor*; the de-
ferving *Favourite*, the *Wild Goofe Chace*, (at the
Black-friers) the *Wedding*; the *Renegado*; the
fair Maid of the *VVeſt*; *Hannibal and Scipio*;
King John and Matilda; (at the Cockpit) and
Holland's Leaguer, (at Salisbury Court.)

Lovew. Thefe are but few indeed : But pray
Sir, what Maſter Parts can you remember
the Old *Black-friers* Men to Act, in *Johnſon*,
Shakeſpear, and *Fletcher*'s Plays.

Trum. What I can at preſent recollect I'll
tell you; *Shakeſpear*, (who as I have heard,
was a much better Poet, than Player) *Burbadge*,
Hemmings, and others of the Older ſort, were
Dead before I knew the Town ; but in my
time, before the Wars, *Lowin* uſed to Act,
with mighty Applauſe, *Falſtaffe*, *Moroſe*, *Vul-
pone*, and *Mammon* in the *Alchymiſt*; *Melan-
cius* in the *Maid's* Tragedy, and at the ſame
time *Amyntor* was Play'd by *Stephen Hammerton*,
(who was at firſt a moſt noted and beautiful
Woman Actor, but afterwards he acted with
equal Grace and Applauſe , a Young Lover's Part) *Tayler* Acted *Hamlet* incomparably
well, *Jago*, *Truewit* in the *Silent Woman*, and
Face in the *Alchymiſt*; *Swanſton* uſed to Play
Othello : *Pollard*, and *Robinſon* were Comedians, ſo was *Shank* who uſed to Act Sir *Roger*,
in the *Scornful Lady.* Theſe were of the *Black-
friers.* Thoſe of principal Note at the *Cockpit*,
were, *Perkins*, *Michael Bowyer*, *Sumner*, *William Allen*, and *Bird*, eminent Actors. and *Ro-
bins*,

kins a Comedian. Of the other Companies I took little notice.

Lovew. Were there so many Companies?

Trum. Before the Wars, there were in being all these Play-houses at the same time. The *Black-friers*, and *Globe* on the *Bankside*, a Winter and Summer House, belonging to the same Company called the King's Servants ; the *Cockpit* or *Phænix*, in *Drury-lane*, called the Queen's Servants; the private House in *Salisbury-court*, called the Prince's Servants; the *Fortune* near *White-cross-street*, and the *Red Bull* at the upper end of St. *John's-street* : The two last were mostly frequented by Citizens, and the meaner sort of People. All these Companies got Money, and Liv'd in Reputation, especially those of the *Blackfriers*, who were Men of grave and sober Behaviour.

Lovew. Which I admire at; That the Town much less than at present, could then maintain Five Companies, and yet now Two can hardly Subsist.

Trum. Do not wonder, but consider, That tho' the Town was then, perhaps, not much more than half so Populous as now, yet then the Prices were small (there being no Scenes) and better order kept among the Company that came; which made very good People think a Play an Innocent Diversion for an idle Hour or two, the Plays themselves being then, for the most part, more Instructive and Moral. Whereas of late, the Play-houses are so extreamly
                                                                  pestered

peftered with Vizard-masks and their Trade, (occafioning continual Quarrels and Abufes) that many of the more Civilized Part of the Town are uneafy in the Company, and fhun the Theater as they would a Houfe of Scandal. It is an Argument of the worth of the Plays and· Actors, of the laft Age, and eafily inferr'd, that they were much beyond ours in this, to confider that they cou'd fupport themfelves meerly from their own Merit ; the weight of the Matter, and goodnefs of the Action, without Scenes and Machines : Whereas the prefent Plays with all that fhew, can hardly draw an Audience, unlefs there be the additional Invitation of a *Signior Fideli*, a *Monfieur L'abbe*, or fome fuch Foreign Regale expreft in the bottom of the Bill.

Lovew. To wave this Digreffion, I have Read of one *Edward Allin*, a Man fo famed for excellent Action, that among *Ben. Johnfon's* Epigrams, I find one directed to him, full of Encomium, and concluding thus

*Wear this Renown, 'tis juft that who did give
So many Poets Life, by one fhould Live.*

Was he one of the *Black-friers* ?

Trum. Never, as I have heard ; (for he was Dead before my time.) He was Mafter of a Company of his own, for whom he Built the *Fortune* Play-houfe from the Ground, a large, round Brick Building. This is he that grew fo
Rich

Rich that he purchafed a great Eftate in *Sur-rey* and elfewhere; and having no Iffue, he Built and largely endow'd *Dulwich* College, in the Year 1619, for a Mafter, a Warden, Four Fellows, Twelve aged poor People, and Twelve poor Boys, &c. A noble Charity.

Lovew. What kind of Playhoufes had they before the Wars?

Trum. The *Black-friers*, *Cockpit*, and *Salis-bury-court*, were called Private Houfes, and were very fmall to what we fee now. The *Cockpit* was ftanding fince the Reftauration, and *Rhode*'s Company Aƈted there for fome time.

Lovew. I have feen that.

Trum. Then you have feen the other two, in effeƈt; for they were all three Built almoft exaƈtly alike, for Form and Bignefs. Here they had Pits for the Gentry, and Aƈted by Candle-light. The *Globe*, *Fortune* and *Bull*, were large Houfes, and lay partly open to the Weather, and there they alwaies Aƈted by Daylight.

Lovew. But prithee, *Truman*, what became of thefe Players when the Stage was put down, and the Rebellion raifed?

Trum. Moft of 'em, except *Lowin*, *Tayler* and *Pollard*, (who were fuperannuated) went into the King's Army, and like good Men and true, Serv'd their Old Mafter, tho' in a different, yet more honourable, Capacity. *Ro-binfon* was Kill'd at the Taking of a Place (I think

think *Baſing Houſe*) by *Harriſon*, he that was after Hang'd at *Charing-croſs*, who refuſed him Quarter, and Shot him in the Head when he had laid down his Arms; abuſing Scripture at the ſame time, in ſaying, *Curſed is he that doth the Work of the Lord negligently.* *Mohun* was a Captain, (and after the Wars were ended here, ſerved in *Flanders,* where he received Pay as a Major *)* *Hart* was a Lieutenant of Horſe under Sir *Thomas Dalliſon,* in *Prince Rupert's,* Regiment, *Burt* was Cornet in the ſame Troop, and *Shatterel* Quarter-maſter. *Allen* of the *Cockpit,* was a Major, and Quarter Maſter General at *Oxford.* I have not heard of one of theſe Players of any Note that ſided with the other Party, but only *Swanſton,* and he profeſt himſelf a Presbyterian, took up the Trade of a Jeweller, and liv'd in *Aldermanbury,* within the Territory of Father *Calamy.* The reſt either Loſt, or expos'd their Lives for their King. When the Wars were over, and the Royaliſts totally Subdued; moſt of 'em who were left alive gather'd to *London,* and for a Subſiſtence endeavour'd to revive their Old Trade, privately. They made up one Company out of all the Scatter'd Members of Several; and in the Winter before the King's Murder, 1648, They ventured to Act ſome Plays with as much caution and privacy as cou'd be, at the *Cockpit.* They continu'd undiſturbed for three or four Days; but at laſt as they were preſenting the Tragedy

gedy of the *Bloudy Brother*, (in which *Lowin*
Acted Aubrey, *Tayler* Rollo, *Pollard* the Cook,
Burt Latorch, and I think *Hart* Otto) a Party of Foot Souldiers befet the House, furprized
'em about the midle of the Play, and carried
'em away in their habits, not admitting them
to Shift, to *Hatton-houfe* then a Prifon, where
having detain'd them fometime, they Plunder'd
them of their Cloths and let 'em loofe again.
Afterwards in *Oliver*'s time, they ufed to
Act privately, three or four Miles, or more,
out of Town, now here, now there, fometimes in Noblemens Houfes, in particular
Holland-houfe at *Kenfington*, where the Nobility and Gentry who met (but in no great
Numbers) ufed to make a Sum for them,
each giving a broad Peice, or the like. And
Alexander Goffe, the Woman Actor at *Black-
friers*, (who had made himfelf known to Per-
fons of Quality) ufed to be the Jackal and give
notice of Time and Place. At Chriftmafs,
and Bartlemew-fair, they ufed to Bribe the
Officer who Commanded the Guard at *White-
hall*, and were thereupon connived at to Act
for a few Days, at the *Red Bull*; but were
fometimes notwithftanding Difturb'd by Soldiers. Some pickt up a little Money by pub-
lifhing the Copies of Plays never before Printed, but kept up in Manufcript. For inftance,
in the Year 1652, *Beaumont* and *Fletcher's Wild
Goofe Chace* was Printed in Folio, *for the Publick ufe of all the Ingenious*, (as the Title-

C   page

page fays) *and private Benefit of* John Lowin *and* Jofeph Tayler, *Servants to his late Majefty*; and by them Dedicated *To the Honour'd few Lovers of Dramatick Poefy* : Wherein they modeftly intimate their Wants. And that with fufficient Caufe; for whatever they were before the Wars, they were, after, reduced to a neceffitous Condition. *Lowin* in his latter Days, kept an Inn (the three Pidgions) at *Brentford*, where he Dyed very Old, (for he was an Actor of eminent Note in the Reign of K. *James* the firft) and his Poverty was as great as his Age. *Tayler* Dyed at *Richmond* and was there Buried. *Pollard* who Lived Single, and had a Competent Eftate ; Retired to fome Relations he had in the Country, and there ended his Life. *Perkins* and *Sumner* of the *Cockpit*, kept Houfe together at *Clerkenwel*, and were there Buried. Thefe all Dyed fome Years before the Reftauration. What follow'd after, I need not tell you: You can eafily Remember.

Lovew. Yes, prefently after the Reftauration, the King's Players Acted publickly at the *Red Bull* for fome time, and then Removed to a New-built Playhoufe in *Vere-ftreet* by *Claremarket.* There they continued for a Year or two, and then removed to the *Theater Royal* in *Drury-lane*, where they firft made ufe of *Scenes*, which had been a little before introduced upon the publick Stage by Sir *William Davenant* at the *Duke's Old Theater* in *Lin-*

Lincolns-Inn-fields, but afterwards very much improved, with the Addition of curious Machines by Mr. *Betterton* at the New *Theater* in *Dorset-Garden*, to the great Expence and continual Charge of the Players. This much impair'd their Profit o'er what it was before; for I have been inform'd, (by one of 'em) That for several Years next after the Restauration, every whole Sharer in Mr. *Hart*'s Company, got 1000 *l. per an*. About the same time that Scenes first enter'd upon the Stage at *London*, Women were taught to Act their own Parts; since when, we have seen at both Houses several excellent Actresses, justly famed as well for Beauty, as perfect good Action. And some Plays (in particular *The Parson's Wedding*) have been Presented all by Women, as formerly all by Men. Thus it continued for about 20 Years, when Mr. *Hart* and some of the Old Men began to grow weary, and were minded to leave off; then the two Companies thought fit to Unite; but of late, you see, they have thought it no less fit to Divide again, though both Companies keep the same Name of his Majesty's Servants. All this while the Play-house Musick improved Yearly, and is now arrived to greater Perfection than ever I knew it. Yet for all these Advantages, the Reputation of the Stage, and Peoples Affection to it, are much Decay'd. Some were lately severe against it, and would

hardly

hardly allow Stage-Plays fit to be longer permitted. Have you feen Mr. *Collier*'s Book?

Trum. Yes, and his Oppofer's.

Lovew. And what think you?

Trum. In my mind Mr. *Collier*'s Reflections are Pertinent, and True, in the Main; the Book ingenioufly Writ, and well Intended: But he has overfhot himfelf in fome Places; and his Refpondents, perhaps, in more. My affection inclines me not to Engage on either fide, but rather Mediate. If there be Abufes relating to the Stage; (which I think is too apparent) Let the Abufe be reformed, and not the ufe, for that Reafon only, Abolifh'd. 'Twas an Old faying when I was a Boy,

Abfit Abufus non defit totaliter Vfus.

I fhall not run through Mr. *Collier*'s Book ; I will only touch a little on two or three general Notions, in which, I think he may be miftaken. What he urges out of the Primitive Councils, and Fathers of the Church, feems to me to be directed againft the Heathen Plays, which were a fort of Religious Worfhip with them, to the Honour of *Ceres*, *Flora*, or fome of their falfe Deities; they had always a little Altar on their Stages, as appears plain enough from fome places in *Plautus*. And Mr. *Collier* himfelf p. 235. tells us out of *Livy*, that Plays were brought in upon the Score

of

of Religion, to pacify the Gods. No wonder
then, they forbid Chriſtans to be preſent at
them, for it was almoſt the ſame as to be
preſent at their Sacrifices. We muſt alſo obſerve that this was in the Infancy of Chriſti-
anity, when the Church was under ſevere,
and almoſt continual Perſecutions, and when
all its true Members were of moſt ſtrict and
exemplary Lives, ⸝not knowing when they
ſhould be call'd to the Stake, or thrown to
Wild-Beaſts. They communicated Daily, and
expected Death hourly; their thoughts were
intent upon the next World, they abſtain'd almoſt wholy from all Diverſions and pleaſures
(though lawfull and Innocent) in this. Afterwards when Perſecution ceaſed, and the
Church flouriſht, Chriſtians being then freed
from their former Terrors, allow'd themſelves,
at proper times, the lawfull Recreations of
Converſation, and among other (no doubt)
this of Shewes and Repreſentations. After this
time, the Cenſures of the Church indeed,
might be continued, or revived, upon occaſion,
againſt Plays and Players, tho' (in my Opinion) it can not be underſtood generally,
but only againſt ſuch Players who were of
Vicious and Licencious Lives, and repreſented
profane Subjects, inconſiſtant with the Morals
and probity of Manners requiſite to Chriſtians; and frequented chiefly by ſuch looſe and
Debaucht People as were much more apt to
Corrupt than Divert thoſe who aſſociated with
them

them. I fay, I can not think the Canons and Cenfures of the Fathers can be applyed to all Players, *quatenus* Players; for if fo how could Plays be continued among the Chriftians, as they were, of Divine Subjects, and Scriptural Stories? A late French Author Speaking of the Original of the *Hotel De Bourgogne* (a Play-houfe in *Paris*) fays that the ancient Dukes of that Name gave it to the Brotherhood of the Paffion, eftablifhed in the Church of Trinity-Hofpital in the *Rue* S. *Denis*, on condition that they fhould reprefent here Interludes of Devotion: And adds that there have been publick Shews in this Place 600 Years ago. The Spanifh and Portuguize continue ftill to have, for the moft part, fuch Ecclefiaftical Stories, for the Subject of their Plays: And if we may beleive *Gage*, they are Acted in their Churches in *Mexico*, and the Spanifh *Weft-Indies*.

Lovew. That's a great way off, *Truman*; I had rather you would come nearer Home, and confine your difcourfe to Old *England*.

Trum. So I intend. The fame has been done here in *England*; for otherwife how comes it to be prohibited in the 88*th* Canon, among thofe paft in Convocation, 1603. Certain it is that our ancient Plays were of Religious Subjects, and had for their Actors, (if not Priefts) yet Men relating to the Church.

Lovew. How does that appear?

Trum.

Trum. Nothing clearer. *Stow* in his Survey
of *London*, has one Chapter *of the Sports and
Paftimes of old time ufed in this City*, and there
he tells us, That in the Year 1391 *(*which was
15 *R.* 2.*)* a Stage-Play was play'd by the Parifh-
Clerks of *London*, at the *Skinner's-well* befide
Smithfield, which Play continued three Days
together, the King, Queen, and Nobles of the
Realm being prefent. And another was play'd
in the Year 1409 *(*11 *H.* 4.*)* which lafted eight
Days, and was of Matter from the Creation of
the World; whereat was prefent moft part of
the Nobility and Gentry of *England.* Sir *William Dugdale* in his Antiquities of *Warwickfhire*,
p. 116, fpeaking of the *Gray-Friers* (or *Fran-
cifcans*) at *Coventry*, fays, Before the fuppreffion of the Monafteries , this City was very
famous for the Pageants that were play'd therein upon *Corpus-Chrifti* Day; which Pageants
being acted with mighty State and Reverence
by the Friers of this Houfe, had Theatres for
the feveral Scenes very large and high, plac'd
upon Wheels, and drawn to all the eminent
Parts of the City, for the better advantage of
the Spectators; and contain'd the Story of the
New Teftament , compofed in old Englifh
Rhime. An ancient Manufcript of the fame is
now to be feen in the *Cottonian* Library, *Sub
Effig.Vefpat. D.* 8. Since the Reformation, in
Queen *Elizabeth*'s time , Plays were frequently
acted by Quirifters and Singing Boys; and feveral of our old Comedies have printed in the
Title

Title Page, *Acted by the Children of* Paul's, (not the School, but the Church) others, *By the Children of her Majesty's Chappel* ; in particular, *Cinthias Revels*, and the *Poetaster* were play'd by them; who were at that time famous for good Action. Among *Ben. Johnson*'s Epigrams you may find *An Epitaph on S. P.* (Sal. Pavy) *one of the Children of Queen* Elizabeth's *Chappel* ; part of which runs thus,

> *Years he counted scarce Thirteen*
> *When Fates turn'd Cruel,*
> *Yet three fill'd Zodiacks he had been*
> *The Stages Jewell.*
> *And did act (what now we moan)*
> *Old Man so duly,*
> *As, sooth, the* Parcæ *thought him one,*
> *He play'd so truly.*

Some of these Chappel Boys, when they grew Men, became Actors at the *Black-friers* ; such were *Nathan Feild*, and *John Underwood*. Now I can hardly imagine that such Plays and Players as these, are included in the severe Censure of the Councils and Fathers; but such only who are truly within the Character given by *Didacus de Tapia,* cited by Mr. *Collier,* p. 276, *viz. The infamous Playhouse* ; *a place of contradiction to the strictness and sobriety of Religion* ; *a place hated by God, and haunted by the Devil.* And for such I have as great an abhorrance as any Man.

Love-

Lovew. Can you guefs of what Antiquity the reprefenting of Religious Matters, on the Stage, hath been in *England?*

Trum. How long before the Conqueft I know not, but that it was ufed in *London* not long after, appears by *Fitz-Stevens,* an Author who wrote in the Reign of King *Henry* the Second. His Words are, *Londonia pro fpectaculis theatralibus, pro ludis fcenicis, ludos habet fanctiores; Reprefentationes miraculorum, quæ fancti Confeffores operati funt, feu Reprefentationes paffionum quibus claruit conftantia Martyrum.* Of this, the Manufcript which I lately mention'd, in the *Cottonian* Library, is a notable inftance. Sir *William Dugdale* cites this Manufcript, by the Title of *Ludus Coventriæ;* but in the printed Catalogue of that Library, p. 113, it is named thus, *A Collection of Plays in old Englifh Metre.* h. e. *Dramata facra in quibus exhibentur hiftoriæ veteris & N. Teftamenti, introductis quafi in Scenam perfonis illic memoratis, quas fecum invicem colloquentes pro ingenio fingit Poeta. Videntur olim coram populo, five ad inftruendum five ad placendum, a fratibus mendicantibus reprefentata.* It appears by the latter end of the Prologue, that thefe Plays or Interludes, were not only play'd at *Coventry,* but in other Towns and Places upon occafion. And poffibly this may be the fame Play which *Stow* tells us was play'd in the Reign of King *Henry* IV, which lafted for Eight Days. The Book feems by the Character and Language to be at leaft 300 Years

old

old. It begins with a general Prologue, giving the Arguments of 40 Pageants or Gesticulations (which were as so many several Acts or Scenes) representing all the Histories of both Testaments from the Creation, to the choosing of St. *Mathias* to be an Apostle. The Stories of the New Testament are more largely exprest, *viz*. The Annunciation, Nativity, Visitation ; but more especially all Matters relating to the Passion very particularly, the Resurrection, Ascention, the choice of St. *Mathias :* After which is also represented the Assumption, and last Judgment. All these things were treated of in a very homely Style, (as we now think) infinitely below the Dignity of the Subject : But it seems the Gust of that Age was not so nice and delicate in these Matters; the plain and incurious Judgment of our Ancestors, being prepared with favour, and taking every thing by the right and easiest Handle : For example, in the Scene relating to the Visitation.

Maria

Wat Husband of oo thyng pray you most mekely,
I haue knowing that our Cosyn Elizabeth with childe is,
That it please you to go to her hastyly,
If ought we myth comfort her it wer to me blys.

Joseph.

A God sake, is she with childe, she?
Than will her husband Zachary be mery.

In

In Montana they dwelle, fer hence, so mory thr,
In the City of Iuda, I know it verily;
It is hence I trowe myles two a fifty,
We ar like to be wery or we come at the same.
I woie with a good will, blessyd wyff Mary;
Now go we forth then in goddys name, &c.

A little before the Resurrection.

Nunc dormient milites, & veniet anima Christi de inferno, cum Adam *&* Eva, Abraham, John Baptist, *& alijs.*

Anima Christi.

Come forth Adam, and Eve with the,
And all my fryndes that herein be,
In Paradys come forth with me
    In blysse for to dwelle.
The fende of hell that is powr foo
He shall be wrappyd and woundyn in woo:
Fro wo to welth now shall ye go,
    With myrth euer mor to melle.

Adam.

I thank the Lord of thy grete grace
That now is forgiuen my gret trespace,
Now shall we dwellyn in blyssull pace, &c.

The last Scene or Pageant, which represents the Day of Judgment, begins thus.

Michael.

Surgite, All men aryse,
Venite ad judicium,
For now is set the High Justice:
And hath assignyd the day of Dome:

Kepe you redyly to this grett assyse,
Borh grett and small, all and sum,
And of yowr answer you now advise,
What you shail say when that yow com,   &c.

These and such like, were the Plays which in
former Ages were presented publickly: Whether they had any settled and constant Houses, for
that purpose, does not appear; I suppose not. But
it is notorious that in former times there was
hardly ever any Solemn Reception of Princes,
or Noble Persons, but Pageants (that is Stages
Erected in the open Street) were part of the
Entertainment. On which there were Speeches
by one or more Persons, in the nature of Scenes;
and before one of the Speakers must be some
Saint of the same Name with the Party to whom
the Honour is intended. For instance, there
is an ancient Manuscript at *Coventry*, call'd
the *Old Leet Book*, wherein is set down in a
very particular manner, (fo. 168) the Reception of Queen *Margaret*, Wife of *H. 6*,
who came to *Coventry* (and I think, with
her, her young Son Prince *Edward*) on the
Feast of the Exaltation of the Holy-Cross, 35.
H. 6. (*1456)* Many Pageants and Speeches were
made for her Welcome; out of all which,
I shall observe but two or three, in the Old
English, as it is Recorded.

St.

St. *Edward.*

Moder of mekenes, Dame Margarete, princes most excellent,
I King Edward wellcome you with affection cordial,
Certefying to your highnes mekely upn entent,
For the wele of the King and you hertily pray I shall,
And for prince Edward my gostly chylde, who I love principal.
Praying the, John Euangelist, my help therein to be,
On that condition right humbly I giue this Ring to the.

John Evangelist.

Holy Edward crowned King, Brother in Clerginity,
My power plainly I will prefer thy will to amplefy.
Most excellent princes of wymen mortal, your Bedeman will I be.
I know your Life so vertuous that God is pleased thereby
The birth of you unto this Reme shall cause great Melody :
The vertuous voice of Prince Edward shall dayly well encrease,
St. Edward his Godfader and I shall prey therefore doubtlesse.

St. *Margaret.*

Most notabul Princes of wymen earthle
Dame Margarete, the chefe myrth of this Empyre,
Ye be hertely welcome to this Cyte.
To the plesure of your highnesse I wyll set my desyre ;
Both nature and gentlenesse doth me require,
Seth we be both of one name, to shew you kindnesse ;
Wherfore by my power ye shall haue no distresse.

I shall pray to the Prince that is endlese
To socour you with solas of his high grace ;
Ye will here my petition this is doubtlesse,
For I wrought all my life that his will wace.
Therefore, Lady, when you be in any dredfull case,
Call on me boldly, thereof I pray you,
And trust in me feythfully, I will do that may pay you.

In the next Reign (as appears in the san
Book, fo. 221) an other Prince *Edward*, So.

O3

of King *Edward* the 4, came to *Coventry* on the 28 of *April*, 14 *E.* 4, (1474) and was entertain'd with many Pageants and Speeches, among which I shall observe only two; one was of St. *Edward* again, who was then made to speak thus,

Noble Prince Edward, my Cousin and my Knight,
And very Prince of our Line com yn dissent,
I Saint Edward have pursued for your faders imperial Right,
Whereof he was excluded by full furious intent.
Unto this your Chamber as Prince full excellent
We be right welcome. Thanked be Crist of his sonde,
For that that was ours is now in your faders honde.

The other Speech was from St. *George*; and thus saith the Book.

———— Also upon the Condite in the Croschepyng was St. George armed, and a kings daughter kneling afore him with a Lamb, and the fader and the moder being in a Towre abowen beholdyng St. George saving their daughter from the Dragon, and the Condite renning wine in four places, and Minstralcy of Organ playing, and St. George having this Speech underwritten.

O mighty God our all succour celestiall
Which this Royme hath given in dower
To thi moder, and to me George protection perpetuall
It to defend from enimys fer and nere,
And as this mayden defended was here
By thy grace from this Dragons devour,
So, Lord preserve this noble prince, and ever be his socour.

Lover. I perceive these holy Matters consisted very much of Praying; but I pitty poor St. *Edward* the Confessor, who in the compass of a few

few Years, was made to promise his favour and assistance to two young Princes of the same Name indeed, but of as different and opposite Interests as the two Poles. I know not how he could perform to both.

Trum. Alas! they were both unhappy, notwithstanding these fine Shews and seeming caresses of Fortune, being both murder'd, one by the Hand, the other by the procurement of *Rich.* Duke of *Glocester.* I will produce but one Example more of this sort of Action, or Representations, and that is of later time, and an Instance of much higher Nature than any yet mentioned, It was at the marriage of Prince *Arthur*, eldest Son of King *Henry* 7. to the Princess *Catherine* of *Spain*, *An.* 1501. Her passage through *London* was very magnificent, as I have read it described in an old M. S. Chronicle of that time. The Pageants and Speeches were many; the Persons represented St. *Catherine*, St. *Ursula*, a Senator, Noblesse, Virtue, an Angel, King *Alphonse*, *Job*, *Boetius*, &c. among others one is thus described, ———— When this Spech was ended, she held on her way tyll she cam unto the Standard in Chepe, where was ordeyned the fifth Pagend made like an hevyn, theryn syttyng a Personage representing the father of hevyn, beyng all formyd of Gold, and brennyng beffor his trone vii Candylls of war standyng in vii Candylstykis of Gold, the said personage beyng envicroned wyth sundry Gyrarchies off Angelis, and syttyng in a Cope of most riïy cloth of Tyssu, garnishyd wyth stoon and perle in most sumptuous wyse. For again whïch sain said Pagend upon the sowth syde of the strete stood at that tyme, in a hows wheryn that tyme dwellyd William Geffrey habyrdasher, the king, the Quene, my Lady the Kingys moder, my, Lord of Oxynfford, wyth many othir Lordys and Ladys, and Perys of this Realm, wyth also certayn Ambassadors of France lately sent from the Frensh King: and so passyng the said Estatys, eyther guyvyng to other due and convenyent Sa-luts and Countenans, so sone as hyr grace was approchid unto the sayd Pagend, the ladyr be-gan his Spech as folowyth.

Hunc veneram locum, septeno lumine septum.
Dignumque Arthuri *totidem Astra micant.*

I am begynyng and ende, that made ech creature
My sylfe, and for my sylfe, but man esspecially
Both male and female, made aftyr myne aun fygure,
Whom I joyned togydyr in Matrimony
And that in Paradyse, declaring oppenly
That men shall weddyng in my Chyrch solempnize,
Fygurid and signifyed by the erthly Paradyse.

In thys my Chyrch I am allway recydent
As my chyeff tabernacle, and most chosyn place,
Among these goldyn Candylstikkis which represent
My Catholyk Chyrch, shynyng affor my face,
With lyght of feyth, wisdom, doctryne, and grace,
And mervelously eke endamyd toward me
Wyth the extyngwible fyre of Charyte.

Wherefore my welbelovid dowgthyr Katharyn,
Syth I have made yow to myne awn semblance
In my Chyrch to be maried, and your noble Childryn
To regn in this land as in their enherytance,
Se that ye have me in speciall remembrance:
Love me and my Chyrch yowr spiritual modyr,
For ye dispysing that on, despyse that othyr.

Look

Look that ye walk in my precepts, and obey them well:
And here I give yow the same blyssyng that I
Gave my well beloved chylder of Israell;
Blyssyd be the fruyt of your bely;
Power substance and fruyts I shall encrease and multyply;
Power rebellious Enimyes I shall put in yowr hand,
Encreasing in honour both yow and yowr land.

Lovew. This would be cenſured now a days as profane to the higeſt degree.

Trum. No doubt on't: Yet you ſee there was a time when People were not ſo nicely cenſorious in theſe Matters, but were willing to take things in the beſt ſence; and then this was thought a noble Entertainment for the greateſt King in *Europe* (ſuch I eſteem King *H.* 7. at that time) and proper for that Day of mighty Joy and Triumph. And I muſt farther obſerve out of the Lord *Bacon*'s Hiſtory of *H.* 7. that the chief Man who had the care of that Days Proceedings was Biſhop *Fox*, a grave Councelor for War or Peace, and alſo a good Surveyor of Works, and a good Maſter of Cerimonies. and it ſeems he approv'd it. The ſaid Lord *Bacon* tells us farther, That whoſoever had thoſe Toys in compiling, they were not altogether Pedantical.

Lovew. Theſe things however are far from that which we underſtand by the name of a Play.

Trum. It may be ſo; but theſe were the Plays of thoſe times. Afterwards in the Reign of K. *H.* 8. both the Subject and Form of theſe Plays began to alter, and have ſince varied more and

E   more

more. I have by me, a thing called *A merry Play betwene the Pardoner and the Frere, the Curate and Neybour Pratte.* Printed the 5 of *April* 1533. which was 24 *H.* 8. (a few Years before the Diffolution of Monafteries) The defign of this Play was to redicule Friers and Pardoners. Of which I'll give you a tafte. To begin it, the Fryer enters with thefe Words,

> Deus hic; the holy Trynyte
> Preferue all that now here be.
> Dere bretherne, yf ye wyll confyder.
> The Caufe why I am com hyder,
> He wolde be glad to knowe my entent;
> For I com not hyther for mony nor for rent,
> I com not hyther for meat nor for meale,
> But I com hyther for your Soules heale, &c.

After a long Preamble, he adreffes himfelf to Preach, when the Pardoner enters with thefe Words,

> God and St. Leonarde fend ye all his grace
> As many as ben affembled in this place, &c

And makes a long Speech, fhewing his Bulls and his Reliques, in order to fell his Pardons for the raifing fome Money towards the rebuilding,

> Of the holy Chappell of fweet faynt Leonarde
> Which late by fyre was deftroyed and marde.

Both thefe fpeaking together, with continual interruption, at laft they fall together by the Ears. Here the Curate enters (for you muft know the Scene lies in the Church)

Hold

Hold your hands; a vengeance on ye both two
That euer ye came hyther to make this ado,
To polute my Chyrche, &c.

Fri. Mayster Parson, I maruayll ye will giue Lycence
To this false knaue in this Audience
To publish his ragman rolles with lyes.
I desyred hym ywys more than ones or twyse
To hold hys pees tyll that I had done,
But he wolde here no more than the man in the mone.

Pard. Why sholde I suffre the more than thou me?
Mayster parson gaue me lycence before the.
And I wolde thou knowyest it I haue relykes here.
Other maner stuffe than thou dost bere:
I wyll edefy more with the syght of it,
Than will all thy pratynge of holy wryt;
For that except that the precher himselfe lyue well
His predycacyon wyll helpe neuer a dell, &c.

Pars. No more of this wranglyng in my Chyrch:
I shrewe your hertys bothe for this lurche.
Is there any blood shed here between these knaues?
Thanked be god they had no staues,
Nor egetooles, for then it had ben wronge.
Well, ye shall synge another songe.

Here he calls his Neighbour *Prat* the Constable, with design to apprehend 'em, and set 'em
in the Stocks. But the Frier and Pardoner
prove sturdy, and will not be stockt, but fall upon the poor Parson and Constable, and bang
'em both so well-favour'dly, that at last they
are glad to let 'em go at liberty: And so the
Farce ends with a drawn Battail. Such as this
were the Plays of that *Age*, acted in Gentle-

mens

mens Halls at Chriſtmaſs, or ſuch like feſtival times, by the Servants of the Family, or Strowlers who went about and made it a Trade. It is not unlikely that * Lords in thoſe days, and Perſons of eminent Quality, had their ſeveral Gangs of Players, as ſome have now of Fidlers, to whom they give Cloaks and Badges. The firſt Comedy that I have ſeen that looks like regular, is *Gammer Gurton's Needle*, writ I think in the reign of King *Edward* 6. This is compoſed of five Acts, the Scenes unbroken, and the unities of Time and Place duly obſerved. It was acted at *Chriſt* Colledge in *Cambridge*; there not being as yet any ſettled and publick Theaters.

* Till the 25 Year of Queen *Elizabeth*, the Queen had not any Players; but in that Year 12 of the beſt of all thoſe who belonged to ſeveral Lords, where choſen & ſworn her Servants, as Grooms, of the Chamber. Stow's *Annals*, p. 698.

Lovew. I obſerve, *Truman*, from what you have ſaid, that Plays in *England* had a beginning much like thoſe of *Greece*, the Monologues and the Pageants drawn from place to place on Wheels, anſwer exactly to the Cart of *Thespis*, and the Improvements have been by ſuch little ſteps and degrees as among the Ancients, till at laſt, to uſe the Words of Sir *George Buck* (in his *Third Univerſity of* England) *Dramatick Poeſy is ſo lively expreſt and repreſented upon the publick Stages and Theatres of this City, as* Rome *in the* Auge *(the higheſt pitch) of her Pomp and Glory, never ſaw it better perfom'd, I mean* (ſays he) *in*
reſpect

respect of the Action and Art, and not of the Cost and Sumptiousness. This he writ about the Year 1631. But can you inform me *Truman*, when publick Theaters were first erected for this purpose in *London?*

Trum. Not certainly; but I presume about the beginning of Queen *Elizabeths* Reign. For *Stow* in his Survey of *London* (which Book was first printed in the Year 1598) says, *Of late Years in place of these Stage-plays* (i. e. those of Religious Matters *) have been used Comedies, Tragedies, Interludes, and Histories, both true and feigned; for the acting whereof certain publick Places, as the Theatre, the Curtine,* &c. *have been erected.* And the continuator of *Stows* Annals, p.1004, says, That in Sixty Years before the publication of that Book (which was *An. Dom.* 1629) no less than 17 publick Stages, or common Playhouses, had been built in and about *London.* In which number he reckons five Inns or Common Osteries, to have been in his time turned into Playhouses, one Cock-pit, St. *Paul*'s finging School, one in the *Blackfriers*, one in the *Whitefriers*, and one in former time at *Newington* Buts; and adds, before the space of 60 Years past, I never knew, heard, or read, of any such Theaters, set Stages, or Playhouses, as have been purposely built within Man's Memory.

Lovew. After all, I have been told, that Stage-Plays are inconsistant with the Laws of this Kingdom, and Players made Rogues by Statute.

Trum.

Tram. He that told you fo ftrain'd a point of Truth. I never met with any Law wholly to fupprefs them : Sometimes indeed they have been prohibited for a Seafon; as in times of *Lent,* general Mourning or publick Calamities, or upon other occafions, when the Government faw fit. Thus by Proclamation, 7 of *April,* in the firft Year of Queen *Elizabeth,* Plays and Interludes were forbid till *Alhallow-tide* next following. *Hollinfhed,* p. 1184. Some Statutes have been made for their Regulation or Reformation, not general fuppreffion. By the Stat. 39 *Eliz.* c. 4. (which was made *for the fuppreffing of Rogues, Vagabonds and fturdy Beggars)* it is enacted, S. 2, 𝕿𝖍𝖆𝖙 𝖆𝖑𝖑 𝖕𝖊𝖗𝖘𝖔𝖓𝖘 𝖙𝖍𝖆𝖙 𝖇𝖊, 𝖔𝖗 𝖚𝖙𝖙𝖊𝖗 𝖙𝖍𝖊𝖒𝖘𝖊𝖑𝖛𝖊𝖘 𝖙𝖔 𝖇𝖊, 𝕻𝖗𝖔𝖈𝖙𝖔𝖗𝖘, 𝕻𝖗𝖔𝖈𝖚𝖗𝖊𝖗𝖘, 𝕻𝖆𝖙𝖊𝖓𝖙 𝖌𝖆𝖙𝖍𝖊𝖗𝖊𝖗𝖘, 𝖔𝖗 𝕮𝖔𝖑𝖑𝖊𝖈𝖙𝖔𝖗𝖘 𝖋𝖔𝖗 𝕲𝖔𝖆𝖑𝖘, 𝕻𝖗𝖎𝖘𝖔𝖓𝖘 𝖔𝖗 𝕳𝖔𝖘𝖕𝖎𝖙𝖆𝖑𝖘, 𝖔𝖗 𝕱𝖊𝖓𝖈𝖊𝖗𝖘, 𝕭𝖆𝖗𝖊𝖜𝖆𝖗𝖉𝖘, 𝖈𝖔𝖒𝖒𝖔𝖓 𝖕𝖑𝖆𝖞𝖊𝖗𝖘 𝖔𝖋 𝕴𝖓𝖙𝖊𝖗𝖑𝖚𝖉𝖊𝖘 𝖆𝖓𝖉 𝕸𝖎𝖓𝖘𝖙𝖗𝖊𝖑𝖘, 𝖜𝖆𝖓𝖉𝖗𝖎𝖓𝖌 𝖆𝖇𝖗𝖔𝖆𝖉, (𝖔𝖙𝖍𝖊𝖗 𝖙𝖍𝖆𝖓 𝕻𝖑𝖆𝖞𝖊𝖗𝖘 𝖔𝖋 𝕴𝖓𝖙𝖊𝖗𝖑𝖚𝖉𝖊𝖘 𝖇𝖊𝖑𝖔𝖓𝖌𝖎𝖓𝖌 𝖙𝖔 𝖆𝖓𝖞 𝕭𝖆𝖗𝖔𝖓 𝖔𝖋 𝖙𝖍𝖎𝖘 𝕽𝖊𝖆𝖑𝖒, 𝖔𝖗 𝖆𝖓𝖞 𝖔𝖙𝖍𝖊𝖗 𝖍𝖔𝖓𝖔𝖚𝖗𝖆𝖇𝖑𝖊 𝕻𝖊𝖗𝖘𝖔𝖓𝖆𝖌𝖊 𝖔𝖋 𝖌𝖗𝖊𝖆𝖙𝖊𝖗 𝕯𝖊𝖌𝖗𝖊𝖊, 𝖙𝖔 𝖇𝖊 𝖆𝖚𝖙𝖍𝖔𝖗𝖎𝖟𝖊𝖉 𝖙𝖔 𝖕𝖑𝖆𝖞 𝖚𝖓𝖉𝖊𝖗 𝖙𝖍𝖊 𝕳𝖆𝖓𝖉 𝖆𝖓𝖉 𝕾𝖊𝖆𝖑 𝖔𝖋 𝕬𝖗𝖒𝖘 𝖔𝖋 𝖘𝖚𝖈𝖍 𝕭𝖆𝖗𝖔𝖓 𝖔𝖗 𝕻𝖊𝖗𝖘𝖔𝖓𝖆𝖌𝖊) 𝕬𝖑𝖑 𝕵𝖚𝖌𝖑𝖊𝖗𝖘, 𝕿𝖎𝖓𝖐𝖊𝖗𝖘, 𝕻𝖊𝖉𝖑𝖊𝖗𝖘 𝖆𝖓𝖉 𝕻𝖊𝖙𝖙𝖞 𝖈𝖍𝖆𝖕𝖒𝖊𝖓, 𝖜𝖆𝖓𝖉𝖊𝖗𝖎𝖓𝖌 𝖆𝖇𝖗𝖔𝖆𝖉, 𝖆𝖑𝖑 𝖜𝖆𝖓𝖉𝖗𝖎𝖓𝖌 𝕻𝖊𝖗𝖘𝖔𝖓𝖘, &𝖈. 𝖆𝖇𝖑𝖊 𝖎𝖓 𝕭𝖔𝖉𝖞, 𝖚𝖘𝖎𝖓𝖌 𝖑𝖔𝖞𝖙𝖊𝖗𝖎𝖓𝖌, 𝖆𝖓𝖉 𝖗𝖊𝖋𝖚𝖘𝖎𝖓𝖌 𝖙𝖔 𝖜𝖔𝖗𝖐 𝖋𝖔𝖗 𝖘𝖚𝖈𝖍 𝖗𝖊𝖆𝖘𝖔𝖓𝖆𝖇𝖑𝖊 𝖂𝖆𝖌𝖊𝖘 𝖆𝖘 𝖎𝖘 𝖈𝖔𝖒𝖒𝖔𝖓𝖑𝖞 𝖌𝖎𝖛𝖊𝖓, &𝖈. 𝕿𝖍𝖊𝖘𝖊 𝖘𝖍𝖆𝖑𝖑 𝖇𝖊 𝖆𝖏𝖚𝖉𝖌𝖊𝖉 𝖆𝖓𝖉 𝖉𝖊𝖊𝖒𝖊𝖉 𝕽𝖔𝖌𝖚𝖊𝖘, 𝖁𝖆𝖌𝖆𝖇𝖔𝖓𝖉𝖘 𝖆𝖓𝖉 𝖘𝖙𝖚𝖗𝖉𝖞 𝕭𝖊𝖌𝖌𝖆𝖗𝖘, 𝖆𝖓𝖉 𝖕𝖚𝖓𝖎𝖘𝖍𝖊𝖉 𝖆𝖘 𝖘𝖚𝖈𝖍.

Lovew. But this priviledge of Authorifing or Licenfing, is taken away by the Stat. 1 *Ja.* 1. ch. 7. S. 1. and therefore all of them (as Mr. *Collier*

lier says, p. 242) are expresly brought under the foresaid Penalty, without distinction.

Trum. If he means all Players without distinction, 'tis a great Mistake. For the force of the Queens Statute extends only to *wandring Players*, and not to such as are the King or Queen's Servants, and establisht in settled Houses by Royal Authority. On such, the ill Character of vagrant Players (or as they are now called, Strolers) can cast no more aspersion, than the wandring Proctors, in the same Statute mentioned, on those of *Doctors-Commons*. By a Stat. made 3. *Ja.* 1. ch. 21. It was enacted, That if any person shall in any Stage-play, Enterlude, Shew, Maygame or Pageant, jestingly or prophanely speak or use the holy name of God, Christ Jesus, the holy Ghost, or of the Trinity, he shall forfeit for every such offence, 10 l. The Stat. 1. *Char.* 1. ch. 1. enacts, That no Meetings, Assemblies, or concourse of People shall be out of their own Parishes, on the Lords day, for any Sports or Pastimes whatsoever, nor any Bear-bating, Bull-bating, Enterludes, Common Plays, or other unlawful Exercises and Pastimes used by any person or persons within their own Parishes. These are all the Statutes that I can think of relating to the Stage and Players; but nothing to suppress them totally, till the two Ordinances of the Long Parliament, one of the 22 of *October* 1647, the other of the 11 of *Feb.* 1647. By which all Stage-Plays and Interludes are absolutely forbid; the Stages, Seats, Galleries, &c. to be pulled down; all Players tho' calling themselves the King or

Queens

Quee..., Servants, if convicted of acting within two Months before such Conviction, to be punished as Rogues according to Law; the Money received by them to go to the Poor of the Parish; and every Spectator to Pay 5 s. to the use of the Poor. Also Cock-fighting was prohibited by one of *Oliver's* Acts of 31 *Mar.* 1654. But I suppose no body pretends these things to be **Laws**; I could say more on this Subject, but I must break off here, and leave you, *Lovewit*; my Occasions require it.

Love. Farewel, Old *Cavalier.*

Trum. 'Tis properly said; we are almost all of us, now, gone and forgoten.

F I N I S.

Roscius Anglicanus,

OR AN

HISTORICAL

REVIEW OF THE

STAGE:

After it had been Suppres'd by means of the late Unhappy Civil War, begun in 1641, till the Time of, King *Charles* the II^s. Restoration in *May* 1660. Giving an Account of its Rise again; of the Time and Places the Governours of both the Companies first Erected their Theatres.

The Names of the Principal Actors and Actresses, who Perform'd in the Chiefest Plays in each House. With the Names of the most taking Plays; and Modern Poets. For the space of 46 Years, and during the Reign of Three Kings, and part of our present Sovereign Lady Queen *A N N E,* from 1660, to 1706.

Non Audita narro, sed Comperta.

London Printed and sold by *H. Playford,* at his House in *Arundel-street,* near the Water-side, 1708.

ERRATA.

Page 2, *Read* Reeves, *for* Knight. P. 9 *r.* Cidaria, *for* Ciduria. P. 19, *line* 33, *r.* Four *for* Three. P. 12, *r.* Aquilius, *for* Aquitius. P. 28 *line* 17, *r.* Moleire, *for* Moleiro. P. 31 *line* 20, *leave out* John, *and r.* Wife of Mr. Antony Leigh. P. 35 *line* 2, *leave out* was, *between* all *and* things. P. 32, *line* 15 *r.* Sir Symon Softhead, *for* Simeon Lofthead.

TO THE
READER.

THE Editor of the ensuing Rela-tion, being long Converfant with the Plays and Actors of the Ori-ginal Company, under the Patent of Sir William Davenant, *at his Thea-tre in* Lincolns-Inn-Fields, *Open'd there* 1662. *And as Book-keeper and Prompter, continu'd fo, till* October 1706. *He Writing out all the Parts in each Play; and Attending every Morning the Actors Rehearfals, and their Performances in Afternoons; Em-boldens him to affirm, he is not very Erronious in his Relation. But as to the Actors of* Drury-Lane *Company,*

under

To the Reader.

under Mr. Thomas Killigrew, *he having the Account from* Mr. Charles Booth *fometimes Book-keeper there ; If he a little Deviates, as to the Succeffive Order, and exact time of their Plays Performances , He begs Pardon of the Reader, and Subfcribes himfelf,*

His very Humble Servant,

John Downes.

Rofcius

Roscius Anglicanus,

OR AN

HISTORICAL REVIEW

OF THE

STAGE.

IN the Reign of King *Charles* the First, there were Six Play Houses allow'd in Town: The *Black - Fryars* Company, His Majesty's Servants; The Bull in St. *John's-street*; another in *Salisbury Court*; another call'd the *Fortune*; another at the *Globe*; and the Sixth at the Cock-Pit in *Drury-Lane*; all which continu'd Acting till the beginning of the said Civil Wars. The scattered Remnant of several of these Houses, upon King *Charles*'s Restoration, Fram'd a Company who Acted again at the Bull, and Built them a New House in *Gibbon's Tennis Court* in *Clare-Market*; in which Two Places they continu'd Acting all 1660, 1661, 1662 and part of 1663. In this time they Built them a New Theatre in *Drury Lane*: Mr *Thomas Killigrew* gaining a Patent from the King in

order

order to Create them the King's Servants; and from that time, they call'd themselves his Majesty's Company of Comedians in *Drury-Lane*.

Whose Names were, *viz.*

Mr. *Theophilus Bird.*	Mr. *Robert Shatterel.*
Mr. *Hart.*	Mr. *William Shatterel.*
Mr. *Mohun.*	Mr. *Duke.*
Mr. *Lacy.*	Mr. *Hancock.*
Mr. *Burt.*	Mr. *Kynaston.*
Mr. *Cartwright.*	Mr. *Wintersel.*
Mr. *Clun.*	Mr. *Bateman.*
Mr. *Baxter.*	Mr. *Blagden.*

Note, these following came not into the Company, till after they had begun in *Drury-Lane*.

Mr. *Hains.*	These Four were Bred up from Boys, under the Master **ACTORS.**
Mr. *Griffin.*	
Mr. *Goodman.*	
Mr. *Lyddoll.*	Mr. *Bell.*
Mr. *Charleton.*	Mr. *Reeves.*
Mr. *Sherly.*	Mr. *Hughs.*
Mr. *Beeston.*	Mr. *Harris.*

Women.

Mrs. *Corey.*	*N O T E,* these following came into the Company some few Years after.
Mrs. *Ann Marshall.*	
Mrs. *Eastland.*	
Mrs. *Weaver.*	
Mrs. *Uphill.*	Mrs. *Boutel.*
Mrs. *Knep.*	Mrs. *Ellin Gwin.*
Mrs. *Hughs.*	Mrs. *James.*
	Mrs. *Rebecca*

| Mrs. *Rebecca Marshall.* | Mrs. *Verjuice.* |
| Mrs. *Rutter.* | Mrs. *Knight.* |

The Company being thus Compleat, they open'd the New Theatre in *Drury-Lane*, on *Thurſday* in *Eaſter* Week, being the 8*th*, Day of *April* 1663, With the Humorous Lieutenant.
Note, this Comedy was Acted Twelve Days Succeſſively.

I.

The Humorous Lieutenant.

King,	Mr. *Winterſel.*
Demetrius,	Mr. *Hart.*
Seleucus,	Mr. *Burt.*
Leontius,	Major *Mohun.*
Lieutenant,	Mr. *Clun.*
Celia,	Mr. *Marſhal.*

II.

Rule a Wife, and have a Wife.

Don Leon,	Major *Mohun.*
Don John Decaſtrio,	Mr. *Burt.*
Michael Perez,	Mr. *Hart.*
Cacafago,	Mr. *Clun.*
Margareta,	Mrs. *Ann Marſhal.*
Eſtifania,	Mrs. *Boutell.*

III.

The Fox.

B 2

Volpone,

Volpone,	Major *Mohun.*
Mosca,	Mr. *Hart.*
Corbachio,	Mr. *Cartwright.*
Voltore,	Mr. *Shatterel.*
Corvino,	Mr. *Burt.*
Sir Politique Woud-be,	Mr. *Lacy.*
Peregrine,	Mr. *Kynaston.*
Lady Woud-be,	Mrs. *Corey.*
Celia,	Mrs. *Marshal.*

IV.

The Silent Woman.

Morose,	Mr. *Cartwright.*
True-Wit,	Major *Mohun.*
Cleremont,	Mr. *Burt.*
Dauphin,	Mr. *Kynaston.*
Sir Amorous,	Mr. *Wintersel.*
Sir John Daw.	Mr. *Shatterel.*
Captain Otter,	Mr. *Lacy,*
Epicene,	Mrs. *Knep.*
Lady Haughty,	Mrs. *Rutter.*
Mrs. Otter.	Mrs. *Corey.*

V.

The Alchemist.

Subtil,	Mr. *Wintersel.*
Face,	Major *Mohun.*
Sir Ep. Mammon,	Mr. *Cartwright.*
Surly,	Mr. *Burt.*
Ananias,	Mr. *Lacy.*

Wholesome

Wholesome,	Mr. *Bateman.*
Dol. Common,	Mrs. *Corey.*
Dame Plyant,	Mrs. *Rutter.*

VI.

The Maids Tragedy.

King,	Mr. *Winterſel.*
Melantius,	Major *Mohun.*
Amintor,	Mr. *Hart.*
Calianax,	Mr. *Shatterel.*
Evadne,	Mrs. *Marſhal.*
Aſpatia,	Mrs. *Boutel.*

VII.

King and no King.

Arbaces,	Mr. *Hart.*
Tygranes,	Mr. *Burt.*
Mardonius,	Major *Mohun.*
Gobrias,	Mr. *Winterſel,*
Lygones,	Mr. *Cartwright.*
Beſſus,	Mr. *Shotterel.*
Arane,	Mrs. *Corey,*
Panthea.	Madam *Gwin.*

VIII.

Rollo, Duke of *Normandy.*

Rollo,	Mr. *Hart.*
Otto,	Mr. *Kynaſton.*
Aubrey,	Major *Mohun.*

B 3   La Torch

La Torch,	Mr. *Burt.*
Dutchefs,	Mrs. *Corey.*
Edith,	Mrs. *Marfhal.*

X.

The Scornful Lady.

Elder Lovelefs,	Mr. *Burt.*
Younger Lovelefs,	Mr. *Kynafton.*
Welford,	Mr. *Hart.*
Sir Roger,	Mr. *Lacy.*
The Lady,	Mrs. *Marfhal.*
Martha,	Mrs. *Rutter.*
Abigail,	Mrs. *Corey.*

XI.

The Elder Brother.

Charles,	Mr. *Burt.*
Euftace,	Mr. *Kynafton.*
Their Father,	Mr. *Loveday.*
The Uncle,	Mr. *Gradwel.*
Charles's Man,	Mr. *Shotterel.*
Lady,	Mrs. *Rutter.*
Lilia Bianca,	Mrs. *Boutel.*

XII.

The Moor of *Venice.*

Brabantio,	Mr. *Cartwright.*
Moor,	Mr. *Burt.*
Caffio,	Mr *Hart.*

Jago

Jago,	Major *Mohun.*
Roderigo,	Mr. *Beeston.*
Desdemona,	Mrs. *Hughs.*
Emilia,	Mrs. *Rutter.*

XIII.

King *Henry* the Fourth.

King,	Mr. *Wintersel.*
Prince,	Mr. *Burt.*
Hotspur,	Mr. *Hart.*
Falstaff,	Mr. *Cartwright.*
Poyns,	Mr. *Shotterel.*

XIV.

The Maiden Queen.

Lysimantes,	Mr. *Burt.*
Philocles,	Major *Mohun.*
Celadon,	Mr. *Hart.*
Queen,	Mrs. *Marshal.*
Asteria,	Mr. *Knep.*
Florimel,	Mrs. *Elen. Gwin.*
Melissa,	Mrs. *Corey.*

XV·

Mock Astrologer.

Don Alonzo,	Mr. *Wintersel.*
Don Lopez,	Mr. *Burt.*
Belamy,	Major *Mohun.*
Wildblood,	Mr. *Hart.*

B 4   Maskal,

Maskal,	Mr. *Shatterel.*
Theodosia,	Mrs. *Hughs.*
Jacyntha,	Mrs. *Elen. Gwin.*
Aurelia,	Mrs. *Quyn.*

XV.

Julius Cæsar.

Julius Cæsar,	Mr. *Bell.*
Cassius,	Major *Mohun.*
Brutus,	Mr. *Hart.*
Anthony,	Mr. *Kynaſton.*
Calphurnia,	Mrs. *Marſhal.*
Portia,	Mrs. *Corbet.*

Note, That theſe being their **Principal Old Stock** Plays; yet in this Interval from the Day they begun, there were divers others Acted,

As
Cataline's Conſpiracy.
The Merry Wives of *Windſor.*
The Opportunity.
The Example.
The Jovial Crew.
Philaſter.
The Cardinal.
Bartholomew-Fair.
The Chances.
The Widow.
The Devil's an Aſs.
Argulus and *Parthenia.*
Every Man in his Humour.
Every Man out of Humour.
The Carnival.
Sejanus.

The

The Merry Devil of *Edmunton.*
Vittoria Corumbona.
As | The Beggars Bush.
The Traytor.
Titus Andronicus.

These being Old Plays, were Acted but now and then ; yet being well Perform'd, were very Satisfactory to the Town.

Next follow the Plays, Writ by the then *Modern Poets,* As,

The *Indian* Emperour.

Emperour,	Major *Mohun.*
Odmar,	*Mr. Winterſel.*
Guymor,	*Mr. Kynaſton.*
Prieſt,	*Mr. Cartwright.*
Cortez,	*Mr. Hart.*
Vaſquez,	*Mr. Burt.*
Ciduria,	*Mrs. Ellen Gwin.*
Almeria,	*Mrs. Marſnall.*

Plain Dealer.

Manly,	*Mr. Hart.*
Freeman,	*Mr. Kynaſton.*
Verniſh,	*Mr. Griffin.*
Novel,	*Mr. Clark.*
Major Oldfox,	*Mr. Cartwright.*
Lord Plauſible,	*Mr. Haines.*

Jerry

Jerry Blackacre, . | Mr. *Charleton.*

Women:

Olivia, | Mrs. *Marshall.*
Fidelia, | Mrs. *Boutel.*
Eliza, | Mrs. *Knep.*
Widow Blackacre, | Mrs. *Corey.*

Tyrannick Love.

Maximin, | Major *Mohun.*
Porphyrius, | Mr. *Hart.*
Placidius, | Mr. *Kynaston.*
Nigrinus, | Mr. *Beeston.*
Amariel, | Mr. *Bell.*
Charinus, | Mr. *Harris.*
Valerius, | Mr. *Lydal.*
Albinus, | Mr. *Littlewood.*
Apollonius, | Mr. *Cartwright.*

Women.

Empress, | Mrs. *Marshall.*
Valeria, | Mrs. *Ellin Gwin.*
St. Catherine, | Mrs. *Boutel.*
Nacur, | Mrs. *Knep.*
Damilcar, | Mrs. *James.*

Aureng Zeb.

Old Emperour, | Major *Mohun.*
Aureng Zeb *his Son,* | Mr. *Hart.*
Moral *the Younger Son,* | Mr. *Kynaston.*
Arimant. | Mr. *Wintersel.*

Women.

Women.

Nourmahal *the Empress*,	Mrs. *Marshal.*
Indamora,	Mrs. *Cox*.
Melesinda,	Mrs. *Corbet.*

Alexander the Great.

Alexander,	Mr. *Hart.*
Clytus,	Major *Mohun.*
Lysimachus,	Mr. *Griffin.*
Hephestion,	Mr. *Clark.*
Cassander,	Mr. *Kynaston.*
Polyperchon.	Mr. *Goodman.*

Women.

Sysigambis,	Mrs. *Corey.*
Statyra,	Mrs. *Boutell.*
Roxana,	Mrs. *Marshall.*

All for Love, or the World well Lost.

Marc Anthony,	Mr. *Hart.*
Ventidius *his General*,	Major *Mohun.*
Dolabella *his Friend*,	Mr. *Clark.*
Alexas *the Queens Eunuch*,	Mr. *Goodman.*
Seraphion,	Mr. *Griffin.*

Women.

Cleopatra,	Mrs. *Boutell.*
Octavia,	Mrs. *Corey.*

The

The Aſſignation, or Love in a Nun-nery.

Duke of Mantua,	Major *Mohun.*
Prince Frederick,	Mr. *Kynaſton.*
Aurelian,	Mr. *Hart.*
Camillo *his Friend,*	Mr. *Burt.*
Mario,	Mr. *Cartwright,*
Aſcanio *Page,*	Mr. *Reeves.*
Benito,	Mr. *Haines,*

Women.

Sophronia,	Mrs. *James.*
Lucretia,	Mrs. *Marſhall.*
Hyppolita *a Nun,*	Mrs. *Knep.*
Laura,	Mrs. *Boutel.*
Violetta,	Mrs. *Cox.*

Mythridates King of *Pontus.*

Mythridates,	Major *Mohun.*
Ziphares,	Mr. *Hart.*
Pharnaces,	Mr. *Goodman,*
Archelaus,	Mr. *Griffin.*
Pelopidus,	Mr. *Winterſel.*
Aquitius,	Mr. *Clark.*

Women.

Monima,	Mrs. *Corbet.*
Semandra,	Mrs. *Boutel.*

The

The Deſtruction of *Jeruſalem*.

Titus Veſpaſian,	Mr. *Kynaſton*.
Phraartes,	Mr. *Hart*.
Matthias *high Prieſt*.	Major *Mohun*.
John,	Mr. *Cartwright*.

Women.

Clarona D.*to* Matthias,	Mrs. *Boutell*.
Queen Berenice,	Mrs *Marſhall*.

Marriage Alamode.

Polydamus,	Mr. *Winterſel*.
Leonidas,	Mr. *Kynaſton*.
Harmogenes,	Mr. *Cartwright*.
Rhodophil,	Major *Mohun*.
Palamede,	Mr. *Burt*.

Women.

Palmira,	Mrs *Cox*.
Amathea,	Mrs *James*.
Doralice,	Mrs *Marſhall*.
Melantha,	Mrs *Boutell*.

The Unhappy Favourite, or the Earl of *Eſſex*.

The Earl of Eſſex,	Mr. *Clark*.
The E. of Southampton,	Mr *Griffin*.
Lord Burleigh,	Major *Mohun*.

Women.

Queen Elizabeth,	Mrs. *Gwin.*
Countess of Rutland,	Mrs. *Cook.*
Countess of Nottingham,	Mrs. *Corbet.*

The Black Prince.

King Edward the 3*d*,	Major *Mohun.*
King John *of* France,	Mr. *Wintersel.*
The Black Prince,	Mr. *Kynaston.*
Lord Delaware,	Mr. *Hart.*
Count Gueselin,	Mr. *Burt.*
Lord Latimer,	Mr. *Cartwright.*

Women.

Alizia,	Mrs. *Gwin.*
Plantagenet,	Mrs. *Marshall.*
Cleorin,	Mrs. *Corey.*
Valeria *Disguis'd,*	F. *Damport.*
A Lady,	Betty *Damport.*

The Conquest of *Granada*, 2 Parts.

Mahomet Boabdelin } *last King of* Granada, }	Mr. *Kynaston,*
Prince Abdalla,	Mr. *Lydal.*
Abdemelech,	Major *Mohun.*
Abenamar,	Mr. *Cartwright.*
Almanzer,	Mr. *Hart.*
Ferdinand *K.* of Spain,	Mr. *Littlewood.*
Duke of Arcos.	Mr. *Bell.*

Women

Women.

Almahide, *Q. of* Gran.	Mrs. *Ellen Gwin.*
Lindaraxa,	Mrs. *Marshall.*
Benzaida,	Mrs. *Boutell.*
Esperanza,	Mrs. *Reeves.*
Isabella *Q. of* Spain,	Mrs. *James.*

Sophonisba, or *Hanibal's* Overthrow.

Hannibal,	Major *Mohun.*
Maherbal,	Mr. *Burt.*
Bomilcar,	Mr. *Wintersel.*
Scinio,	Mr. *Kynaston.*
Lelius,	Mr. *Lydall.*
Massinissa,	Mr. *Hart.*
Massina,	Mr. *Clark.*

Women.

Sophonisba,	Mrs. *Cox.*
Rosalnida.	Mrs. *Boutel*

Note, All the foregoing, both Old and Modern Plays being the Principal in their Stock and most taking, yet, they Acted divers others, which to Enumerate in order, wou'd tire the Patience of the Reader. *As Country Wife ; Love in a Wood;* St. *Jame's-Park ; Amboina ; The Cheats ; Selindra ; The Surprizal; Vestal Virgin ; The Committee ; Love in a Maze ; The Rehearsal:* In which last, Mr. *Lacy,*

For his Juſt Acting, all gave him due Praiſe,
His Part in the Cheats, Jony Thump, Teg and Bayes,
In theſe Four Excelling ; The Court gave him the Bays.

And many others were Acted by the Old
Company at the Theatre Royal, from the time
they begun, till the Patent deſcended to Mr.
Charles Killigrew, which in 1682, he join'd it to
Dr. *Davenant's* Patent, whoſe Company Acted
then in *Dorſet* Garden, which upon the Union,
were Created the King's Company : After
which, Mr. *Hart* Acted no more, having a Pen-
ſion to the Day of his Death, from the United
Company.

I muſt not Omit to mention the Parts in ſeveral Plays of ſome of the Actors; wherein
they Excell'd in the Performance of them. *Firſt,*
Mr. *Hart,* in the Part of *Arbaces,* in King and
no King ; *Amintor,* in the Maids Tragedy ; *O-*
thello ; Rollo ; Brutus, in *Julius Cæſar ; Alexander,*
towards the latter End of his Acting ; if he
Acted in any one of theſe but once in a Fort-
night, the Houſe was fill'd as at a New Play,
eſpecially *Alexander,* he Acting that with ſuch
Grandeur and Agreeable Majeſty, That one of
the Court was pleas'd to Honour him with
this Commendation ; That *Hart* might Teach
any King on Earth how to Comport himſelf :
He was no leſs Inferior in Comedy ; as *Moſca*
in the Fox ; *Don John* in the Chances, *Wildblood*
in the Mock Aſtrologer ; with ſundry other
Parts. In all the Comedies and Tragedies, he
was concern'd he Perform'd with that Exactneſs
and Perfection, that not any of his Succeſſors
have Equall'd him.

Major

Major *Mohun*, he was Eminent for *Volpone* ; *Face* in the *Alchymist* ; *Melantius* in the Maids Tragedy ; *Mardonius*, in King and no King ; *Cassius*, in *Julius Cæsar* ; *Clytus*, in *Alexander* ; *Mithridates*, &c. An Eminent Poet feeing him Act this laft, vented fuddenly this Saying ; Oh *Mohun, Mohun! Thou little Man of Mettle, if I should Write a* 100 *Plays, I'd Write a Part for thy Mouth* ; in fhort, in all his Parts, he was moft Accurate and Correct.

Mr *Wintersel*, was good in Tragedy, as well as in Comedy, efpecially in Cokes in *Bartholomew Fair* ; that the Famous Comedian *Nokes* came in that part far fhort of him.

Then *Mr. Burt, Shatterel, Cartwright* and feveral other good Actors, but to Particularize their Commendations wou'd be too Tedious ; I refer you therefore to the feveral Books, their Names being there inferted.

Next follows an Account of the Rife and Progreffion, of the Dukes Servants ; under the Patent of Sir *William Davenant* who upon the faid Junction in 1682, remov'd to the Theatre Royal in *Drury-Lane*, and Created the King's Company.

In the Year 1659, General *Monk*, Marching then his Army, out of *Scotland* to *London*. Mr. *Rhodes* a Bookfeller being Wardrobe-Keeper formerly (as I am inform'd) to King *Charles* the Firft's, Company of Comedians in *Black-Friars* ; getting a Licenfe from the then Governing State, fitted up a Houfe then for Acting call'd the *Cock-Pit* in *Drury-Lane*, and in a fhort time Compleated his Company.

Their

Their Names were, *viz.*

Mr. *Betterton.*	*Note,* Thefe fix commonly
Mr. *Sheppy.*	Acted Womens Parts.
Mr. *Lovel.*	Mr. *Kynaſton.*
Mr. *Lilliſton.*	*James Nokes.*
Mr. *Underhill.*	Mr. *Angel.*
Mr. *Turner.*	*William Betterton.*
Mr. *Dixon.*	Mr. *Moſely.*
Robert Nokes.	Mr. *Floid.*

The Plays there Acted were,

The Loyal Subject.
Maid in the Mill
The Wild Goofe Chafe.
The *Spaniſh* Curate.
The Mad Lover.
Pericles, Prince of *Tyre.*
A Wife for a Month.
Rule,Wife and have a Wife.
The *Tamer* Tam'd.
The Unfortunate Lovers.
Aglaura.
Changling.
Bondman. *With divers others.*

Mr. *Betterton,* being then but 22 Years Old,
was highly Applauded for his Acting in all
thefe Plays, but efpecially, For the Loyal Subject; The Mad Lover; *Pericles*; The Bondman: *Deſlores,* in the Changling; his Voice
being then as Audibly ftrong, full and Arti-
culate, as in the Prime of his Acting.

Mr.

Mr. Sheppy Perform'd *Theodore* in the Loyal Subject ; Duke *Altophil*, in the Unfortunate Lovers ; *Asotus*, in the Bondman, and several other Parts very well ; But above all the Changling, with general Satisfaction.

Mr. Kynaston Acted *Arthiope*, in the Unfortunate Lovers ; The Princess in the *Mad* Lover ; *Aglaura* ; *Ismenia*, in the Maid in the Mill ; and several other Womens Parts ; he being then very Young made a Compleat Female Stage Beauty, performing his Parts so well, especially *Arthiope* and *Aglaura*. being Parts greatly moving Compassion and Pity ; that it has since been Disputable among the Judicious, whether any Woman that succeeded him so Sensibly touch'd the Audience as he.

Mr. James Nokes Acted first, The Maid in the Mill ; after him *Mr. Angel* ; *Aminta* in the same Play was Acted by *Mr. William Betterton* (who not long after was Drown'd in Swimming at *Wallingford*) They Acted several other Womens Parts in the said Plays, very Acceptable to the Audience : *Mosely* and *Floid* commonly Acted the Part of a Bawd and Whore.

In this Interim, Sir *William Davenant* gain'd a Patent from the King. and Created Mr. *Betterton* and all the Rest of *Rhodes's* Company, the King's Servants ; who were Sworn by my Lord *Manchester* then Lord Chamberlain, to Serve his Royal Highness the Duke of *York*, at the Theatre in *Lincoln's-Inn Fields*.

Note, *The three following, were new Actors taken in by Sir* William, *to Compleat the Company he had from Mr.* Rhodes.

Mr *Harris*

Mr. *Harris.* | Mr. *Richards.*
Mr. *Price.* | Mr. *Blagden.*

The Five following came not in till almoſt a
Year after they begun.

Mr. *Smith.* | Mr. *Young.*
Mr. *Sandford.* | Mr. *Norris.*
Mr. *Medburn.*

Sir *William Davenant's* Women Ac treſſes were,

Note, Theſe Four being his Principal Aᵭreſ
ſes, he Boarded them at his own Houſe.

Mrs *Davenport.* | Mrs. *Davies.*
Mrs. *Saunderſon.* | Mrs. *Long.*

Mrs. *Ann Gibbs.* | Mrs. *Holden.*
Mrs. *Norris.* | Mrs. *Jennings.*

His Company being now Compleat, Si
William in order to prepare Plays to Open hi
Theatre, it being then a Building in *Lincoln's
Inn Fields,* His Company Rehears'd the Firſ
and Second Part of the Siege of *Rhodes;* an
the Wits at *Pothecaries-Hall:* And in Sprin
1662, Open'd his Houſe with the ſaid Play's
having new Scenes and Decorations, being th
firſt that e're were Introduc'd in *England.* M
Betterton, Acted Soly-man the Magnificent
Mr. *Harris, Alphonſo;* Mr. *Lilliſton, Villerius* 'th
Grand Maſter; Mr *Blagden* the Admiral; M
Davenport, Roxolana; Mrs. *Sanderſon* Ianthe

A

All Parts being Juſtly and Excellently Perform'd ; it continu'd Acting 12 Days without
Interruption with great Applauſe.

The next was the Wits, a Comedy, Writ by
Sir *William Davenant* ; The Part of the Elder
Palatine, Perform'd by *Mr. Betterton* ; The
Younger *Palatine* by *Mr Harris* , Sir *Morgly
Thwack*, by *Mr. Underhill* Lady *Ample*, by *Mrs.
Davenport* : All the other Parts being exact-
ly Perform'd ; it continu'd 8 Days Acting Suc-
ceſſively.

The Tragedy of *Hamlet* ; *Hamlet* being Per-
form'd by *Mr. Betterton*, Sir *William* (having ſeen
Mr. Taylor of the *Black-Fryars* Company Act
it, who being Inſtructed by the Author *Mr.
Shakſepeur*) taught Mr. *Betterton* in every
Particle of it ; which by his exact Perfor-
mance of it, gain'd him Eſteem and Reputati-
on, Superlative to all other Plays. *Horatio* by
Mr. Harris ; The King by *Mr. Lilliſton* ; The
Ghoſt by *Mr. Richards*, (after by *Mr. Medburn*)
Polonius by *Mr. Lovel* ; *Roſencrans* by *Mr. Dixon* ;
Guilderſtern by *Mr. Price* ; 1ſt, Grave-maker, by
Mr. Underhill ; The 2ⁿᵈ, by *Mr. Dacres* ; The
Queen, by *Mrs. Davenport* ; *Ophelia*, by *Mrs.
Sanderſon* : No ſucceeding Tragedy for ſeveral
Years got more Reputation, or Money to the
Company than this.

Love and Honour, wrote by Sir *William Davenant* : This Play was Richly C'oath'd ; The
King giving Mr. *Betterton* his Coronation Suit,
in which, he Acted the Part of Prince *Alva-
ro* ; The Duke of *York* giving Mr. *Harris* his,
who did Prince *Proſpero* ; And my Lord of *Oxford*, gave Mr. *Joſeph Price* his, who did *Lionel*

the

the Duke of *Parma*'s Son ; The Duke was Acted by Mr. *Lilliston* ; *Evandra*, by Mrs. *Davenport*, and all the other Parts being very well done : The Play having a great run, Produc'd to the Company great Gain and Estimation from the Town.

Romeo and *Juliet*, Wrote by Mr. *Shakespear* : *Romeo*, was Acted by Mr. *Harris* ; *Mercutio*, by Mr. *Betterton* ; Count *Paris*, by Mr. *Price* ; The *Fryar*, by Mr. *Richards* ; *Sampson*, by Mr. *Sandford* ; *Gregory*, by Mr. *Underhill* ; *Juliet*, by Mrs. *Saunderson* ; Count *Paris*'s Wife, by Mrs. *Holden*.

Note, There being a Fight and Scuffle in this Play, between the House of *Capulet*, and House of *Paris* ; Mrs. *Holden* Acting his Wife, enter'd in a *Hurry*, Crying, O my Dear *Count* ! She Inadvertently left out, O, in the pronuntiation of the Word *Count* ! giving it a Vehement Accent, put the House into such a Laughter, that *London* Bridge at low Water was silence to it.

This Tragedy of *Romeo* and *Juliet*, was made some time after into a Tragi-comedy. by Mr. *James Howard*, he preserving *Romeo* and *Juliet* alive ; so that when the Tragedy was Reviv'd again 'twas Play'd Alternately, Tragical one Day, and Tragicomical another ; for several Days together.

The Adventures of five Hours, Wrote by the Earl of *Bristol*, and Sir *Samuel Tuke* : This Play being Cloath'd so Excellently Fine in proper Habits, and Acted so justly well. Mr. *Betterton*, Acting *Don Henriq*; Mr. *Harris*, *Antonio* ; Mr. *Young*, *Octavio* ; Mr. *Underhill*, *Diego* ; Mr. *Sandford*, *Ernesto* ; Mr. *Smith*, the *Corrigidor* ; Mr. *Price*, *Silvio* ; Mrs. *Davenport*, *Camilla* ; Mrs.

Betterton,

Betterton, Portia; Mrs. *Long, Flora*. It took Successively 13 Days together, no other Play Intervening.

Twelfth Night, Or what you will ; Wrote by Mr. *Shakespear*, had mighty Success by its well Performance : Sir *Toby Belch*, by Mr. *Betterton* ; Sir *Andrew Ague-Cheek*, by Mr. *Harris* ; *Fool*, by Mr. *Underhill* ; *Malvolio* the Steward, by Mr. *Lovel* ; *Olivia*, by Mrs. *Ann Gibbs* ; All the Parts being justly Acted Crown'd the Play. Note, *It was got up on purpose to be Acted on Twelfth Night*.

The Villain, Written by Major *Thomas Porter* ; this Play by its being well perform'd, had Success extremly beyond the Company's Expectation. Mr. *Betterton*, Acting *Monsieur Brisac*, Mr. *Harris*, *Monsieur Beanpre* ; Governour, Mr. *Lilliston* ; *Bontefeu*, Mr. *Young*.

Maligni, the Villain ; Mr. *Saunford, Coligni* ; the Scriveners Son, by that Inimitable Sprightly Actor, Mr. *Price* ; (especially in this part) *Bellmont*, by Mrs. *Betterton* : It Succeeded 10 Days with a full House, to the last,

The Rivals, A Play, Wrote by Sir *William Davenant* ; having a very Fine Interlude in it, of Vocal and Instrumental Musick, mixt with very Diverting Dances ; Mr. *Price* introducing the Dancing, by a short Comical Prologue, gain'd him an Universal Applause of the Town The Part of *Theocles*, was done by Mr. *Harris* ; *Philander*, by Mr. *Betterton* ; *Cunopes* the Jailor, by Mr. *Underhill* : And all the Womens Parts admirably Acted ; chiefly *Celia*, a Sheperdess being Mad for Love ; especially in Singing several Wild and Mad Songs

My

My Lodging it is on the Cold Ground, &c.
She perform'd that so Charmingly, that not
long after, it Rais'd her from her Bed on
the Cold Ground, to a Bed Royal. The Play
by the Excellent performance; lasted uninter-
ruptly Nine Days, with a full Audience.

King *Henry* the 8*th*, This Play, by Order of
Sir *William Davenant*, was all new Cloath'd in
proper Habits: The King's was new, all the
Lords, the Cardinals, the Bishops, the Doctors,
Proctors, Lawyers, Tip-staves, new Scenes:
The part of the King was so right and justly
done by Mr. *Betterton*, he being Instructed in it
by Sir *William*, who had it from Old Mr. *Lowen*,
that had his Instructions from Mr. *Shakespear*
himself, that I dare and will aver, none can,
or will come near him in this Age, in the performance of that part: Mr. *Harris*'s, performance
of Cardinal *Wolsey*, was little Inferior to that,
he doing it with such just State, Port and
Mein, that I dare affirm, none hitherto has E-
quall'd him: The Duke of *Buckingham*, by Mr.
Smith; *Norfork*, by Mr. *Nokes*; *Suffolk*, by Mr.
Lilliston; Cardinal *Campeius* and *Cranmur*, by Mr.
Medburn; Bishop *Gardiner*, by Mr. *Underbill*;
Earl of *Surry*, by Mr. *Young*; Lord *Sands*, by Mr.
Price; Mrs. *Betterton*, Queen *Catherine*: Every
part by the great Care of Sir *William*, being
exactly perform'd; it being all new Cloath'd
and new Scenes; it continu'd Acting 15 Days
together with general Applause.

Love in a Tub, Wrote by Sir *George Etheridge*;
Mr. *Betterton*, performing Lord *Beauford*; Mr.
Smith, Colonel *Bruce*; Mr. *Norris*, *Lovis*; Mr.
Nokes, Sir *Nickolas Cully*; Mr. *Underbill*, *Palmer*;
                                                    Mr.

Mr. *Saunford*, Wheadle ; Mrs. *Betterton*, *Graciana*; Mrs. *Davies*, *Aurelia* ; Mrs. *Long*, the Widow ; Mr. *Harris*, Sir *Frederick Frollick* ; Mr. *Price*, *Dufoy*.

> Sir Nich'las, *Sir* Fred'rick ; *Widow and* Dufoy, *Were not by any so well done*, Mafoy :

The clean and well performance of this Comedy, got the Company more Reputation and Profit than any preceding Comedy ; the Company taking in a Months time at it 1000*l*.

Cutter of Coleman-street ; Written by Mr. *Abraham Cowley* ; Colonel *Jolly*, perform'd by Mr. *Betterton* ; Old *True-man*, by Mr. *Lovel* ; Young *True-man*, Mr. *Harris* ; *Cutter*, Mr. *Underhill* ; Captain *Worme*, Mr. *Sandford* , Parson *Soaker*, Mr. *Note,* This Play was not a little injurious to the Cavalier Indigent Officers; especially the Character of *Cutter* and *Worm.* *Daeres* ; *Puny*, Mr. *Nokes* ; *Will*. Mr. *Price* ; *Aurelia*, by Mrs. *Betterton* ; *Lucia*, Mrs. *Ann Gibbs* ; Laughing *Jane*, by Mrs *Long* : This Comedy being Acted so perfectly Well and Exact, it was perform'd a whole Week with a full Audience.

The Dutchess of *Malfey* ; Wrote by Mr. *Webster* : Duke *Ferdinand*, Perform'd by Mr. *Harris* : *Bosola*, by Mr. *Betterton* : *Antonio*, Mr. *Smith* : *Cardinal*, Mr. *Young* : Dutchess of *Malfey*, by Mrs. *Betterton* : *Julia*, the *Cardinals* Miſtreſs, by Mrs. *Gibbs* : This Play was so exceeding Excellently *Acted* in all Parts ; chiefly, Duke *Ferdinand* and *Bosola* : It fill'd the Houſe 8 Days Succeſsively, it proving one of the Beſt of Stock Tragedies.

The Tragedy of *Muſtapha*, Wrote by the Earl of *Orrery*. The part of *Solyman* the Magnificent,

cent, was done by Mr. *Betterton* : *Muſtapha*, Mr. *Harris* : *Zanger*, Mr. *Smith* : *Ruſtan*, Mr. *Sandford* : *Pyrrhus*, Mr. *Richards* : Mr. *Young* . *Haly*, Mr. *Cademan* : *Roxolana*, Mrs. *Davenport* : (Afterward Mrs. *Betterton*, and then by one Mrs. *Wiſeman*) Queen of *Hungaria*, Mrs. *Davies*. All the Parts being new Cloath'd with new Scenes, Sir *William*'s great Care of having it perfect and exactly perform'd, it produc'd to himſelf and Company vaſt Profit.

Theſe being all the Principal, which we call'd Stock-Plays ; that were *Acted* from the Time they Open'd the Theatre in 1662, to the beginning of *May*, 1665, at which time the *Plague* began to Rage : The Company ceas'd *Acting* ; till the *Chriſtmaſs* after the Fire in 1666. Yet there were ſeveral other Plays *Acted*, from 1662, to 1665, both Old and Modern : As a Comedy call'd, *A Trick to catch the Old One* : *The* Sparagus *Garden* : *Wit in a Conſtable*. Tu Quoque : *The Tragedy of King* Lear, as Mr. *Shakeſpear* Wrote it ; before it was alter'd by Mr. *Tate*. *The Slighted Maid* : *The Step-Mother*, both Written by Sir *Robert Stapleton* : *Law againſt Lovers*, by Sir *William Davenant*. 'Tis better than it was : *Worſe and Worſe* : Theſe Two Comedies were made out of *Spaniſh*, by the Earl of *Briſtol*. The Ghoſts, Wrote by Mr. *Holden* : *Pandora*, Wrote by Sir *William Killigrew*. The Company ending as I ſaid with *Muſtapha*, in *May* 1665, after a Year and Half's Diſcontinuance ; they by Command began with the ſame Play again at Court : The *Chriſtmaſs* after the Fire in 1666 : And from thence continu'd again to Act at their Theatre in *Lincoln's-Inn-Fields*.
The

The first new Play that was Acted in 1666, was: *The Tragedy of* Cambyses, *King of* Persia, Wrote by Mr. *Settle*: Cambyses, was perform'd by Mr. *Betterton*: Prexaspes the General, by Mr. *Harris*: Prince *Smerdis*, Mr. *Young*: *Mandana*, by Mrs. *Betterton*: All the other Parts, being perfectly well Acted, Succeeded six Days with a full Audience.

After this the Company Reviv'd Three Comedies of Mr. Sherly's, *viz.*

The Grateful Servant.
The Witty Fair One.
The School of Complements.
The Woman's a Weather Cock.

These Plays being perfectly well Perform'd; especially *Dulcino* the Grateful Servant, being Acted by Mrs. *Long*; and the first time she appear'd in Man's Habit, prov'd as Beneficial to the Company, as several succeeding new Plays.

Richard the Third, or the *English* Princess, Wrote by Mr. *Carrol*, was Excellently well Acted in every Part; chiefly, King *Richard*, by Mr. *Betterton*; Duke of *Richmond*, by Mr. *Harris*; Sir *William Stanly*, by Mr. *Smith*, Gain'd them an Additional Estimation, and the Applause from the Town, as well as profit to the whole Company.

King *Henry* the 5th, Wrote by the Earl of *Orrery*. Mr. *Harris*, Acted the King: Mr. *Betterton, Owen Tudor*: Mr. *Smith*, Duke of *Burgundy*: Duke of *Bedford*, Mr. *Lilliston*: Earl of *Warwick*, Mr. *Angel*: *Clermont*, Mr. *Medburn*: Queen, Mrs. *Betterton*. This Play was Splendidly Cloath'd: The King, in the Duke of

York's

York's Coronation Suit: *Owen Tudor*, in King
Charle's: Duke of *Burgundy*, in the Lord of
Oxford's, and the rest all New. It was Excellently Perform'd, and Acted 10 Days Successively.

After this my Lord *Orrery*, Writ Two Comedies: The first call'd *Gusman*; the other Mr.
Anthony Gusman, took very well, the other but
indifferent. There being an odd sort of Duel
in it, between Mr. *Nokes* and Mr. *Angel*, both
Comicks meeting in the Field to fight, one
came Arm'd with a *Blunderbus*, the other with
a *Bow* and *Arrows*.

Sir *Martin Marral*, The Duke of *New-Castle*,
giving Mr. *Dryden* a bare Translation of it, out
of a Comedy of the Famous *French* Poet *Monsieur Moleiro*: He Adapted the Part purposely
for the Mouth of Mr. *Nokes*, and curiously Polishing the whole; Mr. *Smith*, Acting Sir *John
Swallow*; Mr. *Young*, Lord *Dartmouth*; Mr. *Underhill*, Old *Moody*; Mr. *Harris*, *Warner*; Mrs.
Norris, Lady *Dupe*; Mrs. *Millisent*, Madam *Davies*. All the Parts being very Just and Exactly perform'd, 'specially Sir *Martin* and his
Man, Mr. *Smith*, and several others since have
come very near him. but none Equall'd, nor
yet Mr. *Nokes* in Sir *Martin*: This Comedy
was Crown'd with an Excellent Entry: In the
last Act at the Mask, by Mr. *Priest* and Madam
Davies; This, and Love in a Tub, got the Company more Money than any preceding Comedy.

She-Wou'd if She Cou'd, Wrote by Sir *George
Etheridge*; *Courtall*, Acted by Mr. *Smith*: *Freeman*, Mr. *Young*: Sir *Joslin*, Mr. *Harris*: Sir Oliver,

liver, Mr. *Nokes* : *Ariana*, Mrs. *Jenning* : *Gatty*, Mrs. *Davies* : Lady *Cockwood*, Mrs. *Shadwell*. It took well, but Inferior to Love in a Tub.

After this were Acted, The Queen of *Arragon*, and *Cupid's* Revenge.

The Impertinents, or Sullen Lovers, Wrote by Mr. *Shadwell* ; This Comedy being Admirably Acted : Especially, Sir *Positive At-all*, by Mr. *Harris* : Poet *Ninny*, by Mr. *Nokes* : *Woodcock*, by Mr. *Angel* : *Standford* and *Emilia* ; the Sullen Lovers : One by Mr. *Smith*, and the other by Mrs. *Shadwell*. This Play had wonderful Success, being Acted 12 Days together, when our Company were Commanded to *Dover*, in *May* 1670. The King with all his Court, meeting his Sister, the Dutchess of *Orleans* there. This Comedy and Sir *Solomon Single*, pleas'd Madam the Dutchess, and the whole Court extremely. The *French* Court wearing then Excessive short Lac'd Coats ; some Scarlet, some Blew, with Broad waft Belts ; Mr. *Nokes* having at that time one shorter than the *French* Fashion, to Act Sir *Arthur Addle* in ; the Duke of *Monmouth* gave Mr. *Nokes* his Sword and Belt from his Side, and Buckled it on himself, on purpose to Ape the *French* : That Mr. *Nokes* lookt more like a Dreft up Ape, than a Sir *Arthur* : Which upon his first Entrance on the Stage, put the King and Court to an Excessive Laughter ; at which the *French* look'd very Shaggrin. to see themselves Ap'd by such a Buffoon as Sir *Arthur* : Mr. *Nokes* kept the Dukes Sword to his Dying Day

Sir *Soloman Single*, Wrote by Mr *Carrol*, Sir *Solomon* Acted by Mr. *Betterton* : *Peregrine Woodland*

land, by Mr. *Harris*: *Single*, by Mr. *Smith* : Mr. *Wary*, by Mr. *Sandford* : *Timothy*, by Mr. *Underhill* : *Betty*, by Mrs. *Johnson* : *Julia*, Mrs. *Betterson*. The Play being Singularly well *Acted*, it took 12 Days together.

The Woman made a Juſtice: Wrote by Mr. *Betterton* : Mrs. *Long*, *Acting* the Juſtice ſo Charmingly ; and the Comedy being perfect and juſtly *Acted*, ſo well pleas'd the Audience, it continu'd *Acting* 14 Days together : The Prologue being ſpoke to it each Day.

The Amorous Widow, or the Wanton Wife, Wrote by the ſame Author. Mr. *Betterton*, Acted *Lovemore* : Mr. *Smith*, *Cunnigham* : Mr. *Nokes*, *Barnaby Brittle* : The Widow, Mrs. *Betterton* : Mrs. *Long*, Mrs. *Brittle* : She Perform'd it ſo well, that none Equall'd her but Mrs. *Bracegirdle*.

The Unjuſt Judge, or *Appius Virginia*, done by the ſame Author. *Virginius Acted* by Mr. *Betterton*, *Appius*, the Unjuſt Judge, by Mr. *Harris* : *Virginia*, by Mrs. *Betterton*. And all the other Parts *Exactly* perform'd, it laſted Succeſſively 8 Days, and very frequently *Acted* afterwards.

The Man's the Maſter, Wrote by Sir *William Davenant*, being the laſt Play he ever Wrote, he Dying preſently after ; and was Bury'd in *Weſtminſter-Abby*, near Mr. *Chaucer's* Monument, Our whole Company attending his Funeral. This Comedy in general was very well Perform'd, eſpecially, the *Maſter*, by Mr. *Harris* ; the *Man*, by Mr. *Underhill* : Mr. *Harris* and Mr. *Sandford*, Singing the Epilogue like two Street Ballad-Singers.

Note,

Note, *Mr.* Cademan *in this Play, not long after
our Company began in* Dorset-Garden ; *his Part being to Fight with Mr.* Harris, *was Unfortunately,
with a sharp Foil pierc'd near the Eye, which so Maim'd
both his Hand and his Speech, that he can make little
use of either ; for which Mischance, he has receiv'd a
Pension ever since* 1673, *being* 35 *Years a goe.*

This being the last New Play that was *Acted*
in *Lincolns-Inn Fields*, yet there were sundry o-
thers done there, from 1662, till the time they
left that House : *As Love's Kingdom,* Wrote by
Mr. Fleckno : The Royal Shepherdess, by *Mr. Shadwell : Two Fools well met,* by *Mr. Lodwick Carlile :
The Coffee-house,* by *Mr. Sincerf : All-Plot, or the
Disguises,* by *Mr. Stroude :* All which Expir'd the
third Day, save the Royal Shepherdess, which
liv'd Six.

Note, About the Year 1670, Mrs. *Aldridge,*
after Mrs. *Lee,* after Lady *Slingsby,* also Mrs.
Leigh Wife, Mr. *John Lee,* Mr *Crosby,* Mrs. *Johnson,* were entertain'd in the Dukes House.

The new Theatre in *Dorset-Garden* being Fi-
nish'd, and our Company after Sir *William's*
Death, being under the Rule and Dominion
of his Widow the Lady *Davenant,* Mr *Betterton,*
and Mr. *Harris,* (Mr. *Charles Davenant*) her
Son *Acting* for her) they remov'd from *Lincolns-
Inn-Fields* thither. And on the Ninth Day of
November 1671, they open'd their new Theatre
with Sir *Martin Marral,* which continu'd *Acting*
3 Days together, with a full Audience each
Day ; notwithstanding it had been *Acted* 30
Days before in *Lincolns-Inn-Fields,* and above 4
times at Court.

Next

Next was *Acted* Love in a Tub, it was performed 2 Days together to a full Audience.

The first new Play *Acted* there, was King *Charles* the VIII. of *France* ; it was all new Cloath'd, yet lasted but 6 Days together, but 'twas *Acted* now and then afterwards.

The next new Comedy, was the *Mamamouchi*, or the Citizen turn'd Gentleman, Wrote by Mr. *Ravenscraft* : *Trickmore*, and Fencing-Master, by Mr *Harris* ; *French* Tutor and Singing Master, by Mr. *Haines* : (He having Affronted Mr. *Hart*, he gave him a Discharge and then came into our House) Old *Jorden*, Mr. *Nokes*; Dr. *Cural*, Mr. *Sandford*; Sir *Simeon Loft-head*, Mr. *Underhill* ; *Lucia*, Mrs. *Betterton* ; *Betty Trickmore*, Mrs. *Leigh*: This Comedy was look upon by the Criticks for a Foolish Play ; yet it continu'd *Acting* 9 Days with a full House ; upon the Sixth the House being very full : The Poet added 2 more Lines to his Epilogue, *viz.*

The Criticks come to Hiss, and Dam this Play,
Yet spite of themselves they can't keep away.

However Mr. *Nokes* in performing the *Mamomouchi* pleas'd the King and Court, next Sir *Martin*, above all Plays.

The third new Play *Acted* there was the Gentleman Dancing-Master, Wrote by Mr. *Witcherly*, it lasted but 6 Days, being like't but indifferently, it was laid by to make Room for other new ones.

Note, *Several of the Old Stock Plays were Acted between each of these 3 new Ones.*

Epsom

Epsom Wells, a Comedy Wrote by Mr. *Shad-well* : Mr. *Rains,* was *Acted* by Mr. *Harris* : *Be-vil,* by Mr. *Betterton* : *Woodly,* by Mr. *Smith* : Justice *Clod-pate,* Mr. *Underhill* : *Carolina,* Mrs. *Johnson* : *Lucia,* Mrs. *Gibbs* : Mrs. *Jilt,* by Mrs. *Betterton* : Mr. *Nokes,* Mr. *Bisket* : Mr. *Angel, Fribble.* This Play in general being Admirably *Acted,* produc'd great Profit to the Company.

Note, *Mrs.* Johnson *in this Comedy, Dancing a Jigg so Charming well, Loves power in a little time after Coerc'd her to Dance more Charming, else-where.*

A Comedy call'd *The Reformation,* Written by a *Master* of Arts in *Cambridge* ; The Reformation in the Play, being the Reverse to the Laws of *Morality* and Virtue ; it quickly made its Exit, to make way for a *Moral* one.

The Tragedy of *Macbeth,* alter'd by Sir *William Davenant* ; being dreft in all it's Finery, as new Cloath's, new Scenes, *Machines,* as flyings for the Witches ; with all the Singing and Dancing in it : T H E first Compos'd by *Mr. Lock,* the other by *Mr. Channell* and *Mr. Joseph Preist* ; it being all Excellently perform'd, being in the nature of an Opera, it Recompenc'd double the Expence ; it proves still a lasting Play.

Note, That this Tragedy, King *Lear* and the *Tempest,* were *Acted* in *Lincolns-Inn-Fields* ; *Lear,* being *Acted* exactly as *Mr. Shakespear* Wrote it ; as likewise the *Tempest* alter'd by Sir *William Davenant* and *Mr. Dryden,* before 'twas made into an Opera.

Loves Jealousy, and *The Morning Ramble.*	Written by *Mr. Nevil Pain.*

Both

Both were very well *Acted*, but after their first run, were laid aside, to make Room for others ; the Company having then plenty of new Poets

The Jealous Bridegroom, Wrote by *Mrs. Bhen*, a good Play and lasted six Days ; but this made its Exit too, to give Room for a greater. *The Tempest*.

Note, *In this Play*, *Mr.* Otway *the Poet having an Inclination to turn Actor* ; *Mrs.* Bhen *gave him the King in the Play, for a Probation Part, but he being not us'd to the Stage ; the full House put him to such a Sweat and Tremendous, Agony, being dash't, spoilt him for an Actor. Mr.* Nat. Lee, *had the same Fate in Acting* Duncan, *in* Macbeth, *ruin'd him for an Actor too. I must not forget my self, being Listed for an Actor in Sir* William Davenant's *Company in* Lincolns-Inn-Fields : *The very first Day of opening the House there, with the Siege of* Rhodes, *being to Act* Haly ; (*The King, Duke of* York, *and all the Nobility in the House, and the first time the King was in a Publick Theatre*) *The sight of that* August *presence, spoil'd me for an Actor too. But being so in the Company of two such Eminent Poets, as they prov'd afterward, made my Disgrace so much the less ; from that time, their Genius set them upon Poetry : The first Wrote* Alcibiades ; *The later, the Tragedy of* Nero ; *the one for the Duke's, the other for the King's House.*

The Year after in 1673. The Tempest, or the Inchanted Island, made into an Opera by *Mr. Shadwell*, having all New in it ; as Scenes, Machines ; particularly, one Scene Painted with *Myriads* of *Ariel* Spirits ; and another flying away, with a Table Furnisht out with Fruits, Sweet meats, and all sorts of Viands ;
just

juſt when Duke *Trinculo* and his Companions,
were going to Dinner ; all was things perform'd in it ſo Admirably well, that not any
ſucceeding Opera got more Money.

About this time the Company was very
much Recruited, having loſt by Death Mr.
Joſeph Price, Mr. *Lovell*, Mr. *Lilliſton*, Mr. *Robert
Nokes*, Mr. *Moſely*, Mr *Coggan*, Mr. *Floid*, Mr.
Gibbons ; Mrs. *Davenport*, Mrs. *Davies*, Mrs. *Jen-
nings*, &c. The three laſt by force of Love
were Erept the Stage : In their Rooms came
in Mr. *Anthony Lee*, Mr. *Gillo*, Mr. *Jevon*, Mr.
Percival, Mr. *Williams*, who came in a Boy, and
ſerv'd Mr. *Harris*, Mr. *Boman* a Boy likewiſe :
Mrs. *Barry*, Mrs. *Currer*, Mrs. *Butler*, Mrs. *Slaugh-
ter*, Mrs. *Knapper*, Mrs. *Twiford*.

After the Tempeſt, came the Siege of *Con-
ſtantinople*. Wrote by Mr. *Nevill Pain*.

Then the Conqueſt of *China* by the *Tartars*,
by Mr. *Settle* ; in this Play Mr. *Jevon* Acting a
Chineſe Prince and Commander in it, and being
in the Battle, Vanquiſht by the *Tartars* ; he
was by his Part to fall upon the point of his
Sword and Kill himſelf, rather than be a Priſo-
ner by the *Tartars* : Mr. *Jevon* inſtead of falling on the point of his Sword, laid it in the
Scabbard at length upon the Ground and fell
upon't, ſaying, now I am Dead ; which put
the Author into ſuch a Fret, it made him ſpeak
Treble, inſtead of Double. *Jevons* anſwer was ;
did not you bid me fall upon my Sword.

In *February* 1673. The long expected Opera of
Pſiche, came forth in all her Ornaments ; new
Scenes, new Machines, new Cloaths, new
French Dances : This Opera was Splendily ſet
out, eſpecially in Scenes ; the Charge of which

amounted to above 800*l.* It had a Continuance of Performance about 8 Days together, it prov'd very Beneficial to the Company ; yet the *Tempest* got them more Money.

After this Sir *Patient Fancy* was Acted.

Then the Rover. Both Wrote by Mrs. *Bhen.*

Alcibiades, the first Play that Mr. *Otway* Wrote.

Madam Fickle, by Mr. *Durfey.*

Then *Don Carlos* Prince of *Spain* ; the Second Play Wrote by Mr. *Otway* : The King, was perform'd by Mr. *Betterton* : Prince, by Mr. *Smith* : *Don John* of *Austria,* by Mr. *Harris* : *Gomez,* Mr. *Medburn* : Queen, Madam *Slingsby* ; and all the Parts being admirably *Acted,* it lasted successively 10 Days ; it got more Money than any preceding Modern Tragedy.

After this in 1676. The Man of *Mode,* or Sir *Fopling Flutter* was *Acted: Dorimant,* by Mr. *Betterton* : *Medly,* Mr. *Harris* : Sir *Fopling,* by Mr. *Smith* : Old *Bellair,* Mr. *Leigh* : Young *Bellair,* Mr. *Jevon* : Mrs. *Lovit,* Mrs. *Barry, Bellinda,* Mrs. *Betterton,* Lady *Woodvil,* Mrs. *Leigh, Emilia,* Mrs. *Twiford* : This Comedy being well Cloath'd and well *Acted,* got a great deal of Money.

The Soldiers Fortune, Wrote by Mr. Otway.

Then the Fond Husband, by Mr. Durfey.

These two. Comedies took extraordinary well, and being perfectly *Acted* ; got the Company great Reputation and Profit.

Circe, an Opera Wrote by Dr. *Davenant* ; *Orestes,* was *Acted* by Mr. *Betterton* : *Pylades,* Mr. *Williams* : *Ithacus,* Mr. *Smith* : *Thoas,* Mr. *Harris* : *Circe,* Lady *Slingsby* : *Iphigenia,* Mrs. *Betterton* : *Osmida,* Mrs. *Twiford.* All the Musick was set by Mr. *Banister,* and being well Perform'd, it

answer'd

answer'd the Expectation of the Company.

The Siege of Troy.　　┐ By Mr. *Banks*.
Anna Bullen.　　　　 ┘

The feign'd Curtezans.　┐ Both by Mrs. *Bhen*.
The City Heiress.　　　┘

　　These Four were well *Acted*; Three of them liv'd but a short time: But *Ann Bullen* prov'd a Stock-Play.

　　Timon of *Athens*, alter'd by Mr. *Shadwell*; 'twas very well *Acted*, and the Musick in't well Perform'd; it wonderfully pleas'd the Court and City; being an Excellent Moral.

　　The Libertine, and Virtuoso: Both Wrote by Mr. *Shadwell*; they were both very well *Acted*, and got the Company great Reputation The *Libertine* perform'd by Mr. *Betterton* Crown'd the Play.

　　The Spanish Fryar, Wrote by Mr. *Dryden*; 'twas Admirably *Acted*, and produc'd vast Profit to the Company.

　　Oedipus King of Thebes, Wrote by Mr. *Nat. Lee*, and Mr. *Dryden*: The last Writing the first two *Acts*, and the first the 3 last This Play was Admirably well *Acted*; especially the Parts of *Oedipus* and *Jocasta*: One by Mr. *Betterton*, the other by Mrs. *Betterton*; it took prodigiously, being *Acted* 10 Days together.

　　The Orphan, or the Unhappy Marriage; Wrote by Mr. *Otway*: *Castalio Acted* by Mr *Betterton*: *Polider*, Mr. *Williams*: *Chamont*, Mr. *Smith*: *Chaplain*, Mr. *Percival*: *Monimia*, Mrs *Barry*: *Serina*, Mrs. *Monfort*. All the Parts being Admirably done, especially the Part of *Monimia*: This

and

and *Belvidera in* Venice preferv'd, *or a Plot Difco-*
ver'd; together with *Ifabella, in the Fatal Mar-*
riage : Thefe three Parts, gain'd her the Name
of Famous *Mrs. Barry*, both at Court and City ; for when ever She *Acted* any of thofe three
Parts, fhe forc'd Tears from the Eyes of her
Auditory, efpecially thofe who have any Senfe
of Pity for the Diftrefs't.

Thefe 3 Plays, by their Excellent performances, took above all the Modern Plays that
fucceeded.

Titus and *Berenice*, Wrote by the fame Author,
confifting of 3 *Acts*: With the *Farce* of the *Cheats*
of *Scapin* at the end : This Play, with the *Farce*,
being perfectly well *Acted*; had good Succefs.

Theodofius, or the *Force of Love*,
Wrote by *Mr. Nathaniel Lee*: *Vara-*
nes, the *Perfian* Prince, *Acted* by
Mr. *Betterton*: *Marcian* the General, Mr. *Smith*: *Theodofius*,
Mr. *Williams*: *Athenais*, Mrs.
Barry: All the Parts in't being
perfectly perform'd, with feve-
ral Entertainments of Singing; Compos'd by
the Famous Mafter Mr. *Henry Purcell*, (being
the firft he e'er Compos'd for the Stage) made
it a living and Gainful Play to the Company :
The Court; efpecially the Ladies, by their
daily charming prefence, gave it great Encour-
agement.

Note, *Mr. Lee*, *Wrote the Tragedy of* Nero. *The Court of* Auguftus, *for Drury-Lane Houfe. The Prince of* Cleve *for Dorfet-Garden, being well Acted, but fucceeded not fo well as the others.*

The *Lancafhire Witches*, *Acted* in 1681, made
by Mr. *Shadwell*, being a kind of Opera, having feveral *Machines* of Flyings for the Witches,
and other Diverting Contrivances in't: All
being well perform'd, it prov'd beyond Expectation;

pectation; very Beneficial to the Poet and
Actors.

All the preceding Plays, being the chief that
were *Acted* in *Dorset-Garden*, from *November*
1671, to the Year 1682; at which time the
Patentees of each Company United Patents;
and by so Incorporating the Duke's Company were made the King's Company, and im-
mediately remov'd to the Theatre Royal in
Drury-Lane.

Upon this Union, Mr. *Hart* being the Heart
of the Company under Mr. *Killigrew's* Patent
never *Acted* more, by reason of his Malady;
being Afflicted with the Stone and Gravel, of
which he Dy'd some time after: Having a
Sallary of 40 Shillings a Week to the Day of
his Death. But the Remnant of that Company; as, Major *Mohun*, Mr *Cartwright*, Mr. *Kynaston*, Mr. *Griffin*, Mr. *Goodman*, Mr. *Duke Wat-
son*, Mr. *Powel* Senior, Mr. *Wiltshire*, Mrs. *Corey*,
Mrs. *Bowtell*, Mrs *Cook*, Mrs. *Monfort*, &c

Note, now Mr. *Monfort* and Mr. *Carlile*, were
grown to the Maturity of good *Actors*

The mixt Company then Reviv'd the several old and Modern Plays, that were the Pro-
priety of Mr. *Killigrew*, as, *Rule a Wife, and have
a Wife*: Mr. *Betterton Acting Michael Perez*: *Don
Leon*, Mr *Smith*: *Cacofogo*, Mr. *Cartwright*: *Mar-
garetta*, Mrs. *Barry*: *Estiphania*, Mrs. *Cook*: Next,

The Scornful Lady.
The Plain Dealer.
The Mock Astrologer.
The Jovial Crew.
The Beggars Bush.

D 4

Par-

Bartholomew-*Fair*.
The Moor of Venice.
Rollo.
The Humorous Lieutenant.
The Double Marriage. With divers others.

Next new Play was the Tragedy of *Valentinian*, wrote by the Lord *Rochester*, from *Beaumont* and *Fletcher*. Mr. *Goodman* Acted *Valentinian*: Mr. *Betterton*, *Æcius*: Mr. *Kynaston*, *Maximus*: Mr. *Griffin*, *Pontius*: Madam *Barry*, *Lucina*, &c. The well performance, and the vast Interest the Author made in Town, Crown'd the Play, with great Gain of Reputation; and Profit to the *Actors*.

In *Anno* 1685: The Opera of *Albion* and *Albianus* was perform'd; wrote by Mr. *Dryden*, and Compos'd by Monsieur *Grabue*: This being perform'd on a very Unlucky Day, being the Day the *Duke* of *Monmouth*, Landed in the *West*: The Nation being in a great Consternation, it was perform'd but Six times, which not Answering half THE Charge they were at, Involv'd the Company very much in Debt.

Note, *Mr.* Griffin *so Excell'd in* Surly. *Sir* Edward Belfond, *The* Plain Dealer, *none succeeding in the 2 former have Equall'd him, except his Predecessor Mr.* Hart *in the latter.*

The first new Comedy after King *James* came to the *Crown*, was Sir *Courtly Nice*, wrote by Mr. *Crown*: Sir *Courtly*, Acted by Mr. *Mounfort*: Hotbead, *Mr.* Underhill: Testimony, Mr. Gillo: Lord *Beaugard*, Mr. *Kynaston*: Surly, by *Mr.* Griffin: Sir *Nicholas Callico*, by the Famous *Mr. Antony Leigh*: Leonora, Madam *Barry*, &c. This Comedy being justly

juſtly *Acted*, and the Characters in't new, Crown'd it with a general Applauſe : Sir *Courtly* was ſo nicely Perform'd, that not any ſucceeding, but Mr. *Cyber* has Equall'd him.

The Squire of *Alſatia*, a Comedy Wrote by Mr. *Shadwell* : Sir *William Belfond*, DONE by Mr. *Leigh* : Sir *Edward*, Mr. *Griffin* : The Squire by Mr. *Nokes*, afterwards by Mr. *Jevon* : *Belfond* Junior, Mr. *Mounfort* : Mrs *Termigant*, Mrs. *Boutel*: *Lucia*, Mrs. *Bracegirdle*. Note, Mr. Leigh was *Eminent in this part of Sir* William, *&* Scapin. *Old* Fumble *Sir* Jolly Jumble. *Mercury in Amphitrion. Sir* Formal. *Spaniſh* Fryar *Pandarus in* Troilus *and* Creſſida. This Play by its Excellent Acting, being often Honour'd with the preſence of Chancellour *Jefferies*, and other great Perſons ; had an Uninterrupted run of 13 Days together.

Note, *The Poet receiv'd for his third Day in the Houſe in* Drury-Lane *at ſingle Prizes* 130*l. which was the greateſt Receipt they ever had at that Houſe at ſingle Prizes.*

About this time, there were ſeveral other new Plays *Acted*. As,

The True Widow.
Sir *Anthony Lone.*
The Scowrers.
Amphytrion.
Love in, and Love out of Faſhion.
Greenwich Park.
Cleomenes.
Troilus and Creſſida.
Cæſar Borgia.

All but *Amphitrion* ; which ſucceeding but indifferently, I Omit the Perſons Names that Acted in this Play ; this proving a Stock-Play.

The

The Old Bachelor, wrote by Mr. *Congreve.*

The Fatal Marriage, or Innocent Adultry; by Mr. *Southern.*

The Double Dealer; by Mr. *Congreve.*

All 3 good Plays; and by their just Performances; specially, Mr. *Doggets* and Madam *Barry's* Unparrell'd.

The Boarding School; Wrote by Mr. *Durfy,* it took well being justly Acted.

The Marriage Hater Match'd, Wrote by the same Author: There Mr. *Dogget* perform'd the part of *Solon* inimitably; likewise his Part in the *Boarding-School.*

King Arthur an Opera, wrote by Mr. *Dryden;* it was Excellently Adorn'd with Scenes and Machines: The Musical Part set by Famous Mr. *Henry Purcel;* and Dances made by Mr. *Jo. Priest:* The Play and Musick pleas'd the Court and City, and being well perform'd, 'twas very Gainful to the Company.

The *Prophetess,* or *Dioclesian* an Opera, wrote by Mr. *Betterton;* being set out with Costly Scenes, Machines and Cloaths: The Vocal and Instrumental Musick, done by Mr. *Purcel;* and Dances by Mr. *Priest;* it gratify'd the Expectation of Court and City; and got the Author great Reputation.

The Fairy Queen, made into an Opera, from a Comedy of Mr. *Shakespears:* This in Ornaments was Superior to the other Two; especially in Cloaths, for all the Singers and Dancers, Scenes, Machines and Decorations, all most profusely set off; and excellently perform', chiefly the Instrumental and Vocal part Compos'

pos'd by the faid Mr. *Purcel*, and Dances by Mr. *Prieſt*. The Court and Town were wonderfully fatisfy'd with it; but the Expences in fetting it out being fo great, the Company got very little by it.

Note, Between thefe Opera's there were feveral other Plays Acted, both Old and Modern. *As*,

Bury Fair.
Wit without Money.
The Taming of a Shrew.
The Maiden Queen.
The Miſtreſs, by Sir Charles Sydly.
Iſland Princeſs.
A Sea Voyage.
The Engliſh *Fryar, by Mr* Crown.
Buſſy D'Ambois.
The Maſſacre of Paris, *&c.*

Some time after, a difference happening between the United Patentees, and the chief *Actors*: As Mr. *Betterton*; Mrs. *Barry* and Mrs. *Bracegirdle*; the latter complaining of Oppreſſion from the former; they for Redreſs, Appeal'd to my Lord of *Dorſet*, then Lord Chamberlain, for Juſtice; who Efpouſing the Cauſe of the Actors, with the aſſiſtance of Sir *Robert Howard*, finding their Complaints juſt, procur'd from King *William*, a Seperate Licenſe for Mr. *Congreve*, Mr. *Betterton*, Mrs. *Bracegirdle* and Mrs. *Barry*, and others, to fet up a new Company, calling it the New Theatre in *Lincoln-Inn-Fields*; and the Houfe being fitted up from a Tennis-Court, they Open'd it the laſt Day of *April*, 1695, with a new Comedy: Call'd,

Love

Love for Love, Wrote by Mr. *Congreve*; this Comedy was Superior in Success, than most of the precedent Plays : *Valentine*, Acted by Mr. *Betterton*; *Scandall*, Mr. *Smith*; *Foresight*, Mr. *Sandford*; *Sampson*, Mr. *Underbill*; *Ben* the Saylor, Mr. *Dogget*; *Jeremy*, Mr. *Bowen*; Mrs. *Frail*, by Madam *Barry*; *Tattle*, Mr. *Boman*; *Angelica*, Mrs. *Bracegirdle*: This Comedy being Extraordinary well Acted, chiefly the Part of *Ben* the Sailor, it took 13 Days Successively.

The Principal new Plays that succeeded this from *April* 1695, to the Year 1704. Were,

Lovers Luck, a Comedy, Wrote by Captain *Dilks*, which fill'd the House 6 Days together, and above 50*l.* the 8*th*, the Day it was left off.

The Grand Cyrus, wrote by Mr. *Banks*; it was a good Play; but Mr. *Smith* having a long part in it, fell Sick upon the Fourth Day and Dy'd, upon that it lay by, and ne'er has bin Acted since.

The Mourning Bride, a Tragedy, wrote by Mr. *Congreve*; had such Success, that it continu'd Acting Uninterrupted 13 Days together.

Boadicea, the Brittish Queen, wrote by Mr. *Hopkins*; 'twas a well Writ Play in an *Ovidean* Stile in Verse; it was lik'd and got the Company Money.

Heroick Love, Wrote by Mr. *George Greenvil*, Superlatively Writ; a very good Tragedy, well Acted, and nightly pleas'd the Court and City.

Lov's a Jest, a Comedy, done by Mr. *Mateox*; succeeded well, being well Acted, and got the Company Reputation and Money.

The Anatomist, or Sham Doctor, had prosperous Success,

Succeſs, and remains a living Play to this Day ; 'twas done by Mr. *Ravenſcroft.*

Don Quixot, both Parts made into one, by *Mr. Durfey,* Mrs. *Bracegirdle* Acting, and her excellent Singing in't ; the Play in general being well Perform'd, 'tis little Inferior to any of the preceding Comedies.

The She-Gallants, a Comedy, wrote by *Mr. George Greenvil,* when he was very Young : Extraordinary Witty, and well Acted ; but offending the Ears of ſome Ladies who ſet up for Chaſtity, it made its Exit. And gave place to,

Iphigenia a Tragedy, wrote by *Mr. Dennis,* a good Tragedy and well Acted ; but anſwer'd not the Expences they were at in Cloathing it.

The Fate of Capua, wrote by *Mr. Southern,* better to Read then Act ; 'twas well Acted, but anſwer'd not the Companies Expectation.

Juſtice Buſy, a Comedy wrote by Mr. *Crown* ; 'twas well *Acted,* yet prov'd not a living Play : However Mrs. *Bracegirdle,* by a Potent and Magnetick Charm in performing a Song in't ; caus'd *the Stones of the Streets to fly in the Men's Faces.*

The Way of the World, a Comedy wrote by Mr. *Congreve,* 'twas curiouſly *Acted* ; Madam *Bracegirdle* performing her Part ſo exactly and juſt, gain'd the Applauſe of Court and City ; but being too Keen a Satyr, had not the Succeſs the Company Expected.

The Ambitious Step-mother, done by Mr. *Rowe* ; 'twas very well *Acted,* eſpecially the Parts of Mr. *Betterton,* Mr. *Booth* and Madam *Barry* ; the Play anſwer'd the Companies expectation

Tamerlane, wrote by the ſame Author, in general

neral well *Acted*; but chiefly the Parts of Mr. *Betterton, Vanbruggen,* Mr. *Powel,* Madam *Bracegirdle* and *Barry*; which made it a Stock-Play.

The Fair Penitent, by the same Author, a very good Play for three *Acts*; but failing in the two last answer'd not their Expectation.

The Biter, a Farce. wrote by the same Author, it had a six Days run; the six Days running it out of Breath, it Sicken'd and Expir'd.

Abra-mule, wrote by Mr. *Trap* of *Oxford*; a very good Play and exceedingly well *Acted.*

These being all the chiefest new Plays, that have been *Acted* by Mr. *Betterton*'s Company, since its Separation from Mr. *Rich* in the Year 1695. The Names of several of the *Actors* I have not mention'd or offer'd to your View, as in the others, by Reason the late *Acting* of them, makes them live in your Memories.

Note, In the space of Ten Years past, Mr. *Betterton* to gratify the desires and Fancies of the Nobility and Gentry; procur'd from Abroad the best Dances and Singers, as, Monsieur *L' Abbe,* Madam *Sublini,* Monsieur *Balon, Margarita Delpine, Maria Gallia* and divers others; who being Exorbitantly Expensive, produc'd small Profit to him and his Company, but vast Gain to themselves; Madam *Delpine* since her Arrival in *England,* by Modest Computation; having got by the Stage and Gentry, above 10000 Guineas

Note, From *Candlemas* 1704, to the 22d, of *April* 1706. There were 4 Plays commanded to be *Acted* at Court at St. *Jame's,* by the *Actors* of both Houses, *viz.*

First, *All for Love*: Mr. *Betterton, Acting Mark. Antony;*

Antony ; Mr. *Vantbrugg*, *Ventidius* ; Mr. *Wilks*, *Dolabella* ; Mr. *Booth*, *Alexas* the Eunuch ; Mrs. *Barry*, *Cleopatra* ; Mrs. *Bracegirdle*, *Octavia* : All the other Parts being exactly done, and the Court very well pleas'd.

The Second was, *Sir* Solomon, *or the Cauticus Coxcomb* : Mr. *Betterton*, Acting *Sir Solomon* ; Mr. *Wilks*, *Peregrine* ; Mr. *Booth*, *Young Single* ; Mr. *Dogget*, Sir *Arthur Addle* ; Mr. *Johnson*, Justice *Wary* ; Mr. *Pinkethman*, *Ralph* ; Mr. *Underhill*, *Timothy* ; Mrs. *Bracegirdle*, *Julia* ; Mrs. *Mounfort*, *Betty* : The whole being well perform'd, it gave great Satisfaction.

The next was, *The Merry Wives of* Windsor, *Acted* the 23d, of *April*, the Queens Coronation Day : Mr. *Betterton*, Acting Sir *John Falstaff* ; Sir *Hugh*, by Mr. *Dogget* ; Mr. *Page*, by Mr. *Vanbruggen* ; Mr. *Ford*, by Mr. *Powel* ; Dr. *Cains*, Mr. *Pinkethman* ; the Host, Mr. *Bullock* ; Mrs. *Page*, Mrs. *Barry* ; Mrs. *Ford*, Mrs. *Bracegirdle* ; Mrs. *Ann Page*, Mrs. *Bradshaw*.

The last was, *The Anatomist*, *or Sham-Doctor* ; it was perform'd on *Shrove-Tuesday*, the Queen's Birth Day, it being done by the *Actors* of both Houses, and perfectly Perform'd ; there being an Additional Entertainment in't of the best Singers and Dancers, Foreign and *English* : As *Margarita D'elpine*, *Maria Gallia*, Mrs. *Lindsey*, Mrs. *Hudson* and Mr. *Leveridge*, and others : The Dances were perform'd by *Monsieur L'Abbe* ; Mr. *Ruel* ; *Monsieur Cherrier* ; Mrs. *Elford* ; Miss *Campion* ; Mrs. *Ruel* and *Devonshire* Girl: 'Twas very well lik'd by the whole Court.

About the end of 1704, Mr. *Betterton* Assign'd his License, and his whole Company over to Captain

Captain *Vanbrugg* to *Act* under HIS, at the Theatre in the *Hay Market*.

And upon the 9*th*, of *April* 1705. Captain *Vanbrugg* open'd his new Theatre in the *Hay-Market*, with a Foreign Opera, Perform'd by a new set of Singers, Arriv'd from *Italy*; (the worst that e're came from thence) for it lasted but 5 Days, and they being lik'd but indifferently by the Gentry; they in a little time marcht back to their own Country.

The first Play *Acted* there, was *The Gamester*. Then the *Wanton Wife*. Next, *Duke and no Duke*. After that, *She wou'd, if She Cou'd*; and half a Score of their old Plays, *Acted* in old Cloaths, the Company brought from *Lincolns-Inn-Fields*. The Audiencies falling off extremly with entertaining the Gentry with such old Ware, whereas, had they Open'd the House at first, with a good new *English* Opera, or a new Play; they wou'd have preserv'd the Favour of Court and City, and gain'd Reputation and Profit to themselves.

The first new Play *Acted* there, Was *the Conquest* of Spain; the beginning of *May* 1705, Written by *Mrs. Pix*, it had not the life of a Stock-Play, for it Expir'd the 6*th*, Day.

The next new one was *Ulysses*, wrote by *Mr. Row*: The Play being all new Cloath'd, and Excellently well perform'd had a Successful run, but fell short of his Ambitious *Step-Mother*, and his *Tamerlane*.

Then was *Acted* a Comedy call'd the *Confederacy*, wrote by Captain *Vanbrugg*, an Excellent Witty Play, and all Parts very well *Acted*: But the Nice *Criticks Censure* was, it wanted just *Decorum*; made it flag at last

Trelooby

Trelooby a Farce, Wrote by Captain *Vantbrugg:* Mr. *Congreve* and Mr. *Walſh,* Mr. *Dogget* Acting *Trelooby* ſo well, the whole was highly Applauded.

The Miſtake, Wrote by Captain *Vantbrugg;* a very diverting Comedy, Witty and good Humour in't, but will ſcarce be Enroll'd a Stock-Play.

The next new Play was, *The Revolution of* Sweden; Wrote by Mrs. *Trotter,* ſhe kept cloſe to the Hiſtory, but wanting the juſt Decorum of Plays, expir'd the Sixth Day.

Then a new Opera call'd, *The Britiſh Enchanters,* Wrote by the Honourable Mr. *George Greenvil;* very Exquiſitly done, eſpecially the Singing Part; making Love the *Acme* of all Terreſtrial Bliſs: Which infinitely arrided both Sexes, and pleas'd the Town as well as any *Engliſh* Modern Opera.

After this was perform'd, an Opera, call'd *The Temple of Love;* conſiſting all of Singing and Dancing: The Singing Compos'd by Monſieur *Sidgeon:* The Verſion into *Engliſh,* by Monſieur *Moteux* from the *Italian:* The Singing perform'd by Mr. *Laurence,* Mr. *Laroon,* Mr. *Cook,* Mrs. *Bracegirdle, Maria Gallia,* and ſeveral other Men and Women for the Chorus's: The Dances, made and perform'd all by *French-*Men; it laſted but Six Days, and anſwer'd not their Expectation.

The laſt Opera was, *The Kingdom of Birds;* made by Mr. *Durfey,* perform'd in *July,* 1706. The Singers in't were, Mr. *Cook,* Mr. *Laroon,* Mr. *Laurence,* Mrs. *Hudſon* and others: Dancers were, Monſieur *De Bargues,* Monſieur *L'Abbe's*

E   Brother,

Brother, Mr. *Fairbank*, Mrs. *Elford* and others: It lasted only Six Days, not answering half the Expences of it.

After this, Captain *Vantbrugg* gave leave to Mr. *Verbruggen* and Mr. *Booth*, and all the Young Company, to Act the remainder of the Summer, what Plays they cou'd by their Industry get up for their own Benefit; continuing till *Bartholomew-Eve*, 23d, of *August*, 1706, ending on that Day, with *The* London *Cuckolds*: But in all that time their Profit Amounted not to half their Salaries, they receiv'd in Winter.

From *Bartholomew* day 1706, to the 15th, of *Octob.* following, there was no more *Acting* there.

In this Interval Captain *Vantbrugg* by Agreement with Mr. *Swinny*, and by the Concurrence of my Lord Chamberlain, Transferr'd and Invested his License and Government of the Theatre to Mr. *Swinny*; who brought with him from Mr. *Rich*, Mr. *Wilks*, Mr. *Cyber*, Mr. *Mills*, Mr. *Johnson*, Mr. *Keene*, Mr. *Norris*, Mr. *Fairbank*, Mrs. *Oldfield* and others; United them to the Old Company; Mr. *Betterton* and Mr. *Underhill*, being the only remains of the Duke of *York*'s Servants, from 1662, till the Union in *October* 1706. Now having given an Account of all the Principal Actors and Plays, down to 1706. I with the said Union, conclude my History.

Next follows the Account of the present Young Company (which United with the Old, in October, 1706.) Now Acting at the Theatre Royal in Drury-Lane; Her Majesty's Company of Comedians, under the Government of Col. Brett.

Mr. *Wilks*,

Mr. *Wilks,* Proper and Comely in Perſon, of Graceful Port, Mein and Air; void of Affectation; his Elevations and Cadencies juſt, Congruent to Elocution: Eſpecially in Gentile Comedy; not Inferior in Tragedy. The Emiſſion of his Words free, eaſy and natural; Attracting attentive ſilence in his Audience, (I mean the Judicious) except where there are Unnatural Rants, As,

――――――――――――― *I'le mount the Sky,*
And kick the G----ds like Foot-balls, as I fly :

As Poet *D----rſy* has it,

Which puts the Voice to ſuch Obſtreperous ſtretch,
Requires the Lungs of a Smith's *Bellows to reach.*

He is indeed the finiſht Copy of his Famous Predeceſſor, Mr. *Charles Hart.*

Mr. *Cyber,* A Gentleman of his time has Arriv'd to an exceeding Perfection, in hitting juſtly the Humour of a ſtarcht Beau, or Fop; as the Lord *Fopington;* Sir *Fopling* and Sir *Courtly,* equalling in the laſt, the late Eminent Mr. *Mounfort,* not much Inferior in Tragedy, had Nature given him Lungs Strenuous to his finiſht Judgment.

Mr. *Eſcourt, Hiſtrio Natus;* he has the Honour (Nature enduing him with an eaſy, free, unaffected Mode of Elocution) in Comedy always to Lætificate his Audience, eſpecially Quality, (Witneſs Serjeant *Kyte*) He's not Excellent only in that, but a Superlative Mimick.　　　　　E 2　　　　　Mr.

Mr. *Booth*, A Gentleman of liberal Education, of form Venuſt ; of Melliſluent Pronuntiation, having proper Geſticulations, which are Graceful Attendants of true Elocution ; of his time a moſt Compleat Tragedian.

Mr. *Johnſon*, He's Skilful in the Art of Painting, which is a great Adjument, very Promovent to the Art of true Elocution, which is always requirable in him, that bears the Name of an Actor ; he has the Happineſs to gain Applauſe from Court and City : Witneſs, *Moroſe*, *Corbaccio*, Mr. *Hothead* and ſeveral others ; He is a true Copy of Mr. *Underhill*, whom Sir *William Davenant* judg'd 40 Year ago in *Lincolns-Inn-Fields*, the trueſt Comedian in his Company.

Mr. *Dogget*. On the Stage, he's very Aſpectabund, wearing a Farce in his Face ; his Thoughts deliberately framing his Utterance Congruous to his Looks : He is the only Comick Original now Extant : Witneſs, *Ben. Solon*, *Nikin*, The *Jew of Venice*, &c.

Mr. *Pinkethman*, He's the darling of *Fortunatus*, he has gain'd more in Theatres and Fairs in Twelve Years, than thoſe that have Tugg'd at the Oar of Acting theſe 50.

Next Mr. *Mills*, Mr. *Powel*, Mr. *Bullock* ; the 2 firſt Excell in Tragedy ; the orher in Comedy, *&c.*

I muſt not Omit Praiſes due to Mr. Betterton, *The firſt and now only remain of the old Stock, of the Company of Sir* William Davenant *in* Lincolns-Inn-Fields ; *he like an old Stately Spreading Oak now ſtands fixt, Environ'd round with brave Young Growing, Flouriſhing Plants : There needs nothing to ſpeak his Fame, more than the following Parts.*

Pericles Prince of *Tyre*.	*Solyman* the Magnificent.
The Bondman.	*Hamlet*.
Cæſar Borgia.	*Macbeth*.
The Loyal Subject.	*Timon* of *Athens*.
The Mad Lover.	*Othello*.
Richard the Third.	*Oedipus*.
King *Lear*.	*Jaffeir*.
	King *Henry* the Eighth.
	Sir John *Falſtaff*.

Mr. *Dryden* a little before his Death in a Prologue, rendring him this P R A I S E.

He like the ſetting Sun, ſtill ſhoots a Glimmery Ray.
Like Antient R O M E *Majeſtick in decay.*

F I N I S.